VISUAL COMMUNICATION

FOR ARCHITECTS AND DESIGNERS:
constructing the persuasive presentation

Margaret Fletcher
ORCID 0000-0002-1630-6640

First published 2021
by Routledge
52 Vanderbilt Avenue, New York, NY 10017

and by Routledge
2 Park Square, Milton Park, Abingdon, Oxon, OX14 4RN

Routledge is an imprint of the Taylor & Francis Group, an informa business

© 2021 Taylor & Francis

The right of Margaret Fletcher to be identified as author of this work has been asserted by her in accordance with sections 77 and 78 of the Copyright, Designs and Patents Act 1988.

All rights reserved. No part of this book may be reprinted or reproduced or utilized in any form or by any electronic, mechanical, or other means, now known or hereafter invented, including photocopying and recording, or in any information storage or retrieval system, without permission in writing from the publishers.

Trademark notice: Product or corporate names may be trademarks or registered trademarks, and are used only for identification and explanation without intent to infringe.

Publisher's Note
This book has been designed by the author and prepared from the provided camera-ready copy.

Library of Congress Cataloging-in-Publication Data
Names: Fletcher, Margaret, 1969– author.
Title: Visual communication for architects and designers : constructing the persuasive presentation / Margaret Fletcher.
Description: New York : Routledge, 2021. | Includes bibliographical references and index.
Identifiers: LCCN 2020023065 (print) | LCCN 2020023066 (ebook) | ISBN 9780367134617 (hardback) | ISBN 9780367134631 (paperback) | ISBN 9780429026621 (ebook)
Subjects: LCSH: Communication in architectural design.
Classification: LCC NA2750 .F56 2021 (print) | LCC NA2750 (ebook) | DDC 729—dc23
LC record available at https://lccn.loc.gov/2020023065
LC ebook record available at https://lccn.loc.gov/2020023066

ISBN: 978-0-367-13461-7 (hbk)
ISBN: 978-0-367-13463-1 (pbk)
ISBN: 978-0-429-02662-1 (ebk)

Typeset in Helvetica Neue, Futura and Gill Sans.

To Russ,
Thank you. . . for everything.

Contents

01
communication, representation and presentation

01 Defining and Integrating the Systems

What is Communication Design?

What is Representation Design?

What is Presentation Design?

How to Develop Your Visual, Verbal and Written Argument: Integrating Communication, Representation and Presentation Design

When to Start Designing the Presentation

11 The Design Narratives

Design Narratives for Presentations

Presentation Narrative: Goals and Purpose

Visual Narrative: Goals and Purpose

Project Narrative: Goals and Purpose

02
constructing a visual argument

15 Developing the Project Narrative
Finding Gaps in the Project Narrative
Order of the Project Narrative
Primary Images and Support Images
Begin Constructing Your Presentation

21 Systems of Visual Structure and Visual Organization
Grid and Alignment Systems
Designing the Layout: Active Area and Margins
Visual Relationship Between Objects on a page

43 Basics of Graphic Design as Related to Presentations
Visual Order and Visual Hierarchy
Typography
Graphic Punctuation

71 Presentation Conventions for Architecture
Symbols and Conventions
Labeling Systems
Visual Legibility of Presentation Drawings
Image Quality Issues

03
presentation design

87 Designing the Presentation Narrative
Building a Complex Argument
In-Person Reviews versus Blind Reviews
Printed Boards versus Digital Slide Decks

99 Designing Boards
Strategies for Board Organization
Common Board Challenges
Setup and Submission

115 Text in Your Presentation: Content and Visual Goals
Three Levels of Reading of a Presentation
What it Says: The Value of Words
How it Looks: The Graphic Presence of Text in Your Presentation
Content and Visual Goals of Text in Your Presentation

127 Strategies for Different Presentation Types
In-Person Presentations
Competitions and Blind Review Presentations
Digital Presentations

04
presenting yourself professionally

135 Cover Letters and Correspondence, Resumes and Portfolios
Cover Letters and Correspondence
Resume Recommendations
Portfolio Design Actions

05
drawing for impact

167 Case Study Examples

276 Notes
277 Acknowledgments
280 Illustration Credits
282 Index

VISUAL COMMUNICATION

FOR ARCHITECTS AND DESIGNERS:
constructing the persuasive presentation

Visual Communication for Architects and Designers teaches you the art of designing a concise, clear, compelling and effective visual and verbal presentation. Margaret Fletcher has developed a reference manual of best practices that gives you the necessary tools to present your work in the best way possible. It includes an impressive 750 presentation examples by over 180 designers from 24 countries in North America, South America, Europe, the Middle East, Asia, Oceania and Africa. This book offers actionable advice to solve a variety of complex presentation challenges.

You will learn how to:

- Understand differences in communication design, representation design and presentation design and know how to use these skills to your advantage;
- Structure the visual and verbal argument in your presentation;
- Design your presentation layouts, architectural competitions, boards and digital presentations;
- Manage issues related to the presentation of architectural and design ideas;
- Present yourself professionally.

Your ability to communicate your design ideas to others is an invaluable and important skill. *Visual Communication for Architects and Designers* shows you how to develop and implement these skills and gain command of your presentations.

Margaret Fletcher is an associate professor of architecture at the College of Architecture, Design and Construction at Auburn University in Auburn, Alabama, USA. She is the author of the companion book, *Constructing the Persuasive Portfolio*.

Introduction

Architectural and design presentations can take many different formats. They can be verbal, visual, analog or digital; they can include images, films, animations, models and anything else you can think of. However, the one thing they all have in common is the ultimate goal of conveying ideas to an audience. The audience may differ and the complexity of ideas may differ but universally this is the goal. The primary challenge with a design presentation is that the argument must be made visually. Simply delivering design ideas verbally allows each audience member to visually conceive of their own solutions in their respective mind's eye. This phenomenon entirely defeats the purpose of a good design argument!

For a visual argument to be successful, it must propose as many questions and it answers. The argument should challenge notions that are customarily accepted. The real question is, how do you do that? That's a tough question and one that can only truly be answered through practice. However, there are some straightforward graphic guidelines that can be followed and leaned upon to help with the conveyance of a clear message. This book aims to make these guidelines available to the designer. Once you add the complexity inherent in a visual, architectural argument, the real challenge begins.

Architectural solutions answer a vast number of design challenges and require multiple streams of representation to begin to address all of the issues that coalesce to generate a successful project. You must be able to identify all of the design opportunities and organize ideas in a hierarchical manner. Even though we understand that the design process is not a linear one, there has to be order to a solution or the reviewers will get twisted up in a complex argument and will never actually see the beauty of the solution. Therefore, it is important to separate the design process from the design ideas.

Focusing on the design ideas will allow order to prevail and will help you begin to organize ideas and divide them into digestible parts to be represented individually. There are opportunities within a presentation to demonstrate the conglomeration of all of the ideas—this typically happens with the primary image(s). Just remember, it is also equally important to be able to break down concepts into understandable pieces so the audience can mentally build and comprehend the complexity that you have been working through.

Ideas and graphic strategies as first described in the companion book, *Constructing the Persuasive Portfolio: The Only Primer You'll Ever Need* are developed further in this publication. The first book in this pair deals exclusively with graphic issues and organizational strategies for portfolio development. As this second book on presentation design was being developed, it became obvious that students were struggling to translate what they understood at the scale of a book—the portfolio—to the scale of any type of larger presentation. Therefore, there are places where content categories deliberately overlap between books— regarding portfolio design and presentation design— and purposefully reinforce these ideas in an effort to make clear the overriding graphic rules that govern all representation objectives.

This publication attempts to elucidate differences and similarities in communication design, representation design and presentation design. As you work through the material, hopefully understanding these differences and similarities will make the dissemination of your own work more productive and powerful.

The visual content for this publication was selected from over 50,000 images submitted for possible inclusion. The final 750 examples offer a detailed view of the work happening around the world at the time of publishing. Students studying in the following countries are represented in the work found in this publication: Australia, Canada, China, Denmark, India, Ireland, Italy, Jordan, Liechtenstein, Mexico, Nepal, Poland, Russia, Singapore, South Africa, South Korea, Spain, Sweden, Sudan, Taiwan, Turkey, the United Arab Emirates, the United Kingdom and the United States of America.

Margaret Fletcher

defining and integrating the systems

communication, representation and presentation

Many types of design processes go into the development of a successful and persuasive presentation. There is a lot to know and learn! Often, we hear the terms communication design, representation design and presentation design used interchangeably but these are distinctly different design devices. All are used to convey ideas but each relies on a different focus and dissemination of specific information. Understanding the differences will help you define what you are already doing and will help you determine what design processes are missing in the advancement of your work.

What is Communication Design?

Effective communication is the exchange of ideas that garners mutual understanding. Persuasive communication allows for the exchange of ideas with the goal of creating a new and authentic understanding.

It all sounds relatively simple. However, in actuality, communication is much more complex than it appears. The communication process involves the delivery of information (this can be designed and controlled) and the reception of information or how material is received and understood (this is not in our control). However, the more we work on the communication of our ideas, the more likely they will be understood as intended.

The ultimate reality is that the message sent may not always be the message received. While we can never completely control how our communication is received, through the understanding of basic principles of communication, it can be managed.

Principles of successful communication design:

1. Know your audience
2. Everything communicates something
3. Delivery matters: clarity is key
4. Complex information is better communicated visually
5. A system and process for feedback is necessary

Know Your Audience

For communication to be successful, it is vital to understand the audience. Imagine delivering a presentation in Spanish to discover the entire audience speaks Korean! While this is an extreme example, it makes a strong point. When you don't know who the audience is, it is impossible to develop your communication approach. It is always best to design your communication strategies with the idea that your audience is completely unfamiliar with your topic. This does not mean that you need to dumb down the material, it simply means that everything must be organized into a complete and clear argument. Do not leave anything out and assume the audience will automatically know what you are talking about. This applies to written, verbal and visual information.

Everything Communicates Something

All images and words communicate. You can't prevent this. Everything conveys a meaning of some sort. The job of the communication designer is to ensure that images and words are communicating what is desired! Ignoring something or leaving something out entirely still communicates a message. But in that case, the designer has decided to relinquish control over the message being delivered and that's never a good idea.

It is also important to understand cultural or professional bias and assumptions when trying to communicate ideas. The understanding of color is a really simple way to master this idea. Everyone recognizes that green in an architectural plan implies landscape of some sort. The color green can also signify environmental issues. These are universal understandings. They will convey meaning whether you intend them to or not. It is important to be aware of these universal symbols and to use them appropriately.

Delivery Matters: Clarity is Key

The communication process relies on the clear and precise delivery of information in a manner that is logical. Start with broad topics and use them to organize the smaller details into a cohesive argument. Verbally begin by outlining what you are going to present and then use that outline as an orienting device throughout the presentation. This helps the person receiving your message to recognize what is coming. It allows them to watch for the very points that will make your argument clear.

It is also a good idea to repeat or relate information. This can be done verbally or visually. Use similar phrasing in titles and captions to relate concepts. Also relate drawings and images to one another visually so the audience can make the intended connections.

Communication, Representation and Presentation—**Defining and Integrating the Systems**

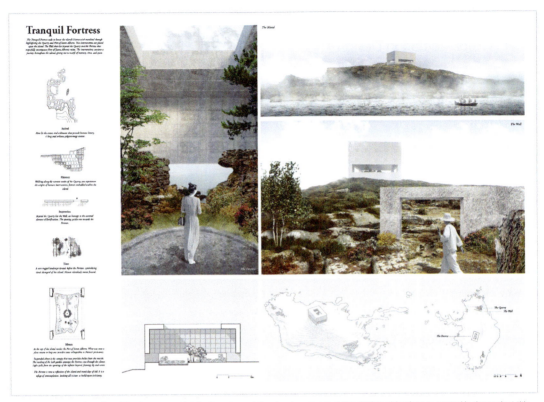

Strong yet ethereal quality of the images and delicate nature of the drawings support the design objectives as stated in the project title. Drawing selections from Tranquil Fortress by Nathan Chen and Andrew Hong.

Complex Information is Better Communicated Visually

Design solutions often generate a multitude of related design problems. The complexity can sometimes become overwhelming. Complex information is understood better if communicated visually. A paragraph verbally describing a spatial condition in the design proposal of an open, light-filled museum is not as compelling as a visual rendering of that space. This holds true for all information. Determine which pieces of your design argument would best be communicated visually; it is likely all of it.

Simply stated, it is easier for a reviewer to retain an image in their mind's eye rather than the image of a piece of text. Giving the reviewer an image to ponder while they are trying to relate additional information will help them make visual and thus, ideological connections.

A System and Process for Feedback is Necessary

The only way to know if what you are trying to communicate is being understood is through feedback. The actual day of the presentation is too late for this type of feedback. Ask others what they think your drawings and images convey. Ask them to listen to your verbal argument and then tell you what they think they heard. Let others critique your use of written words with images to see if the relationships are as you intend. You get the idea. The real message here is. . . get feedback early and get it often. Focus this feedback specifically on the communication of your message.

Visual Communication for Architects and Designers: constructing the persuasive presentation

What is Representation Design?

For the purpose of our discussion regarding presentations, representation design is the creation of visual components of an argument that convey primary ideas through the exploration of graphic portrayals. Project representations can have a variety of visual goals. Great representation design strives to achieve all of these visual goals. Representation design should:

1. Convey meaning
2. Contribute to the clarity of the message
3. Use systems of signs and symbols to represent ideas
4. Demonstrate the hand of the designer
5. Display the perceived truth

Convey Meaning

All project representations must convey meaning. A significant challenge with representation design is to know exactly what needs to be conveyed. For complex design work this can be especially challenging. While working through the design process, it is important to keep a running list of all of the ideas you are trying to develop through the project. Use this list as a guide to determine what ideas need to be conveyed in the representation stage of the project. Bundling design ideas around similar topics will help streamline this process. Keep in mind that a representation without intentional meaning behind it is wasteful. On any given presentation, you will only have a certain amount of space to convey all of your ideas. Don't squander it!

Contribute to the Clarity of the Message

This seems obvious but make sure that the representations you design actually contribute to the clarity of your message. To get this right you will need to enlist the help of some colleagues to give an honest opinion about whether or not what you show actually depicts what you mean. Do this review often and do it early! Remember that everything conveys meaning. Be careful that your graphic choices are not straying from your message.

Use Systems of Signs and Symbols to Represent Ideas

We have established that everything has meaning but certain things have very specific meaning. In the design profession, these systems of signs and symbols are related to things like conventions of architectural drawing—orthographic conventions for plan, section and elevation—or descriptive, graphic signs such as explanatory icons or diagrams. When using these signs and symbols, it is important to remember that they exist for a reason and that reason is so that large numbers of people can read the same drawings and understand them in a similar way. Using them in ways that are not standard can be confusing. Also, failing to use a normative symbol or sign when one is needed can be equally confusing to the delivery of your ideas.

Demonstrate the Hand of the Designer

We have just discussed the importance of using systems of signs and symbols to create universal understanding in representation design. It is equally important that the visual voice of the designer is apparent. There is an opportunity in representation design to develop the look and feel of a piece of representation such that it is uniquely yours. It takes time to establish your own signature representation style and frankly part of the fun of representation design is to explore multiple stylistic options as you are developing your hand. Look to pieces of representation design you admire and try to emulate it. It is impossible to make a direct copy of someone else's design. Your hand will reveal itself as you are trying to replicate the example. That's the beauty of each designer's potential; everything readjusts and is reworked through an individual design process.

Display the Perceived Truth

It could be argued that project representations should only convey the absolute truth. While in theory I am inclined to agree, there are situations in representation design where perceptual understanding is more important than the truth. This can happen when something is technically depicted incorrectly in the digital representation so that a more important idea can be conveyed. This idea becomes important in situations

Communication, Representation and Presentation—**Defining and Integrating the Systems**

Using systems of call-outs and image references strengthens the design argument by relating visual information. Drawing selections from After Nature: Bridging the Grand Metropolitan of Havana by Helena Rong.

where the designer is trying to convey the atmosphere or attitude of a particular space. It may be important to do something like remove a wall in a digital model to get the camera angle just right to show the intended quality of the space. While this is perhaps a view that could never be seen by an occupant, it is a vitally important view to convey the ideas of the project. There are many different ways to describe this idea of perceived truth; remember that the job of the representation designer is first and foremost to convey ideas.

What is Presentation Design?

Presentation design is the purposeful dissemination of complex ideas to an audience with the expressed goal of transferring information, ideas and knowledge. Successful presentations have many things in common but most importantly they should:

1. Convey confidence and enthusiasm
2. Demonstrate knowledge on the subject
3. Connect and resonate with the audience
4. Display logical organization
5. Rely on compelling graphics and words to convey meaning
6. Communicate a practiced message

Convey Confidence and Enthusiasm
It is important when designing your presentation to remember that even if you are not present for the presentation (a blind review) it is imperative that confidence and enthusiasm is displayed through the presentation. If you are doing a verbal presentation this has a lot to do with how you deliver the information verbally. However, the visual presentation must be equally confident and enthusiastic. Visual confidence can come from the strength of your graphic material and it can come from the thoroughness of the thought behind the graphic argument. The display of enthusiasm should hit these marks as well. It will show in the meticulous and comprehensive nature of your presentation.

Demonstrate Knowledge on the Subject
Design the presentation to be thorough. Do not visually skimp or skip material in hopes that you can cover it verbally. Give your ideas presence by having graphic representations there to support what you say or write. An idea that is only briefly mentioned, whether verbally or visually, is fleeting. The job of the presentation is to convey ideas that linger so that the reviewer can understand how the argument is assembled.

Connect and Resonate with the Audience
When giving a verbal presentation, speak from notes rather than reading your presentation. While it is possible to read small segments of text, make sure that you let the audience know you are going to read a bit just so you get it absolutely correct. Then go back to a more conversational style. Keep yourself in the present by attempting to engage in a conversation with your audience. The word "presentation" shouldn't always mean a shiny, polished regurgitation of facts and figures. Connecting and resonating with an audience in a visual way is similar. Use graphic annotations to remind the reviewer of visual connections you are hoping they will make in your graphic argument. Do not make the reviewer work too hard to understand your points either visually or verbally.

Display Logical Organization
Designing your presentation to be organized is a task that works its way up through the developing argument during the entire design process. Spending time trying to organize the order or manner in which you present your argument will help you understand it better. The better you understand your argument, the clearer you will be in the presentation. In both the verbal and visual argument, pack similar material into digestible segments. Relate verbal points to one another and relate visual graphics to one another. Use principles of visual order and visual hierarchy to structure your visual argument into packs of information that can be understood together and in the desired order.

Rely on Compelling Graphics and Words to Convey Meaning
This concept has been discussed in the representation design section of this chapter but is emphasized again here to reiterate the importance that a successful visual presentation is composed of meaningful graphics. It is also crucial to remember that at least some portion of your presentation must be visually compelling. There should be something that visually catches the reviewer's eye and sparks some curiosity. It is an important idea to work some portion of the presentation into this category. Every visual piece does not need to be compelling; some graphics are meant to be visually supportive. Design your presentation such that the compelling graphic material is vital to the conveyance of meaning in your project.

Subtle graphics connected visually within the presentation help the reviewer understand not only the orthographic relationship of the project but also the atmospheric quality of the designed space. Drawing selections from Space for Art by Julia Hager.

Communicate a Practiced Message

Great presentations are practiced presentations. Testing out your argument both visually and verbally is imperative for a successful presentation. However, be very careful that you do not over-practice. Presentations should be designed to be delivered in a natural and conversational manner. Too much practicing can leave the presenter caught in their own head trying to remember where they are in their argument. A visual presentation has to be practiced just as a verbal one does. In a presentation that relies only on visual materials, practicing relies more on colleagues reviewing your graphic material and helping you determine if it conveys a message as intended. Do not ignore any of this practice. It is the process that will most inform you if you are on the right track with your design work.

How to Develop Your Visual, Verbal and Written Argument: Integrating Communication, Representation and Presentation Design

It is already apparent from the characteristic overlaps in the sections defining communication design, representation design and presentation design that these design processes have significant collaborative overlays. So much so that it sometimes can be difficult to determine which design process you are working within. In truth, it's not really important to constantly be aware of whether you are designing the communication, representation, or presentation of your project. However, it is important to know the primary goals of each type of design process and to know that it is necessary to deliberately design within all three systems. To be blissfully unaware of what you are doing is counterproductive when you are putting your design ideas out into the universe in a bid to connect your ideas to the understanding of the audience.

It is certainly a challenge to keep the integration of communication, representation and presentation design in mind throughout the development of a design project. There are so many things to think about just in designing

Visual Communication for Architects and Designers: constructing the persuasive presentation

your actual project. However, it is important to do so. Try this: take the principles defined in each of the previous sections on communication design, representation design and presentation design and consider them holistically. Work through an exercise of combining the lists so that you can package tasks that relate to one another. Then literally post this list in your work area so that you can see it regularly. Keeping a reminder visible at all times is a powerful tool in developing the skills to keep larger, meta tasks (such as these three design strategies) in mind while working on the day-to-day details that drive a complex design project.

When to Start Designing the Presentation

We've already stated that presentation design should not be considered separately from the actual design of your project. The project, whether it will actually be built or not, should be designed to exist primarily in the design presentation. It is here that all of the project ideas will ultimately be tested. If the ideas of the project are not successfully conveyed through presentation, it is as if the ideas—and therefore the project—don't exist at all.

So, how in the world can you design a presentation while simultaneously designing a project? It is simple, really, and will help you immensely in determining which elements of representation and which elements of your project actually need to be designed. Think of it this way, knowing you need to make a display—a presentation—of 2,000 cookies in two weeks helps focus your decisions and tasks. For instance, you won't spend a week and a half working out just how to get cake to fit into a cookie shape; you're not making cake! The same principle applies to design presentations; if you know you need four boards of explanatory diagrams to convey your ideas, you will better know how to direct your energy.

Some people will disagree completely with this method of working. They believe that a designer should thoroughly resolve and design all parts of a project before designing the presentation. In an ideal world,

where there is time to spare, this would be a fantastic idea! However, the truth of the matter is that there is never enough time to design a project fully or even to design what the authors themselves would like to resolve. There is just never enough time. It is very important that designers are realistic about what they can accomplish and are prepared to focus on those representational items that best explain the primary ideas of a project.

With all of that in mind, as soon as you start your design project, start your presentation. Lay out your boards with the basic assumptions of what you think you might need to convey ideas: diagrams, sketches, a large descriptive image, plans, sections, elevations and determine the size and scale these representations will be on the board based on simple math and square footage knowledge. Of course, in the beginning, this will largely be guesswork but week by week the boards can be updated as your work progresses with the representational material you develop. You simply can't know what to focus on if you don't have the end goal of the presentation in mind. There isn't enough time in a design cycle to leave the presentation to the end and, frankly, it makes absolutely no sense. In order to be efficient with design and production, the presentation must be understood from the beginning and undertaken as an integral part of the design process.

This simultaneous process of designing the project and the presentation isn't foolproof. It is entirely possible that everything progresses nicely and at the end you are still met with a design presentation that looks like it is missing some of the most important ideas. To manage this, it is imperative to maintain and develop a list of project artifacts and project ideas as the design progresses. Do your best to stay organized with your ideas, maintaining them in a hierarchical fashion so that you can make sound decisions about the size and placement of representational artifacts within your presentation. You can begin blocking out your presentation very early in the design process as you work through the three design narratives—presentation narrative, visual narrative and project narrative—simultaneously. Understanding how these narratives can impact your daily work is imperative and is discussed in depth in the next chapter

Communication, Representation and Presentation—**Defining and Integrating the Systems**

In order to really get started on your presentation early in the design process you do need to know what kind of review will happen. As mentioned before there are several different types of reviews with the primary categories being an in-person review or a blind review. For either of these situations, the presentation might be printed (boards) or projected (digital). If the presentation is a printed one, find out as soon as possible what the requirements will be. Look for information on size, number and orientation of boards. If the presentation is a digital one, find out if it will be a simple projection of design boards or a more narrative style presentation as can be designed as a slide deck through something like Microsoft PowerPoint.

The final mode of presentation matters. Plans resolved to 1/4" = 1' don't look the same smaller—the design may appear cluttered because of compressed lines and line weight issues—or larger—the design may appear unresolved due to lack of detail in the plan. Line weight and text hierarchy appropriate for print may not work projected or vice versa. In either case, how the presentation looks on a laptop screen is not anywhere close to how it will appear in its final output. Colors shift when printed or projected, line weights look different when printed or projected; even text styles look different. The presentation can only be evaluated if it is viewed in its true, final output form. Don't wait until the end to test the visuals. Test early, test frequently and test smartly.

Working with Tee-up Sets

A tee-up set is essentially a mock-up of your presentation. These are really easy to get started. Once the presentation format is known, simply set the layouts up digitally and block out the types of drawings or representations you plan to have for the project. Go ahead and print this set that just has boxes and words on it. Pin it up and use it as a backdrop to pin up drawings as they are developed. Seeing everything developing while placed together on the presentation tee-up set will really help you determine what needs work. It is ideal to have two or three presentation tee-up sets going at once so that one layout idea does not become the only one. It can be quite difficult to move forward and consider different layout ideas if you've only been looking at just one option throughout the design process.

Working with Digital Slide Decks

It is very important to develop the order of the presentation narrative when preparing for a digital slide deck presentation. This order will ultimately become the outline of the presentation. The outline will shift and change as the project design shifts and changes but keeping this all in mind will eventually prepare you to develop your complete design argument as you move through the design process. A few things you should keep in mind while establishing your digital presentation narrative:

1. It is a good idea to storyboard your slide deck presentation. This storyboard process is very similar to creating a tee-up set to be used for a board presentation. In the case of a slide deck, the storyboard will help establish the order of the argument; a very important element to an argument presented through a linear slide deck.

2. When establishing your storyboard, keep it to one basic idea per slide. Anything more than this and the design argument could get muddy.

A Note on Software

Printed presentations should be designed in layout software such as Adobe InDesign or similar. Use programs such as Adobe Photoshop for editing image raster files (pixel-based), Adobe Illustrator for vector (line and tone) drawings and Microsoft Word for text information. Using the proper software for the appropriate job will make the development and refinement of the presentation a much smoother operation.

the design narratives

communication, representation and presentation

Beginning a design presentation can be a daunting task but it doesn't have to be! First and foremost, it is important to understand that the design presentation is an extension of your project and should be regarded as an opportunity to expose all of your ideas to the reviewers who will ultimately critique your work. Keeping this in mind can help you focus and connect your design intentions to your design actions.

Design presentations come in a variety of different forms. The process for designing each of the different types of presentations is very similar and can produce a wide variety of presentation outcomes. It is critical to know and understand up front the end goals of your presentation and most importantly to know what format your design presentation will take and how it will be reviewed. This will impact how you prepare for your presentation and ensure time and effort isn't wasted.

In an ideal situation, the presentation requirements will be determined and announced at the beginning of the design exercise. However, this is not always the case. In those situations, maintain some flexibility in the way design representations are developed and stay focused on the primary design objectives that need to be conveyed.

Ultimately the presentation will be the most important tool of persuasion to achieve the communication of your project. The design presentation is the only place the project exists if it is an unbuilt project and it is actually the only way to convey your design ideas. It is very important to get the presentation right!

There are several different types of presentations to be aware of. Any of them could be assigned and you should be prepared to address them all. These presentation types can be broken down into two primary categories: physical, in-person presentations—both printed and digitally projected—and blind presentations where the designer is not allowed to give any verbal argument. In this case, the visual representations must do all of the arguing on the behalf of the designer.

Are the types of presentations all that different?
While these two primary categories of presentation—in-person and blind—seem radically different, they really aren't. Often for in-person presentations a lot of ideation content is left for the designer to verbalize during the presentation without a visual representation of that idea. How many times have you heard from a reviewer, "What you are saying sounds really

compelling but there is no evidence of those ideas in the representations of your project in this presentation!" To hear these words during a review is a clear indication that you completely missed the mark on your representation and presentation opportunities.

To avoid this situation, it is best to design your presentation assuming you will not be there to verbally convey ideas. All ideas should be clearly, logically and visually represented in the design presentation; leave nothing in your head. If it is not visually represented in the presentation, it does not exist! Words—written or spoken—should act as support to bolster the legibility of your design ideas that have been visually represented.

An easy way to manage this process is to keep a running list of the design ideas that are shaping your project. As work progresses, this list will gain some ideas, lose some ideas and will certainly be reordered over and over again. It is through this fluctuation of design ideas that a concentrated project narrative emerges. As the content gets more and more focused, make sure that each and every important concept has a visual representation to explain the idea.

As you move forward through the design process, these ideas and visual representations—artifacts—will become more and more refined and more and more ordered. A hierarchy of both design representations and design ideas will develop that will direct you to the appropriate material for your design presentation. It is important to use this system to drive your work forward. Design representations without ideas behind them mean nothing; ideas without design representations to explain them also mean nothing.

Design Narratives for Presentations

There are three readily identifiable design narratives that must be addressed in the design of your project presentation. The three types of narratives are: presentation narrative, visual narrative and project narrative. All three of these systems should be considered as organizational systems for the presentation. Presentation narrative determines the manner in which the project is described or revealed in the presentation. The visual narrative considers issues and systems of a visual nature and spans across the design of the entire presentation. Project narrative specifically refers to all of the parts and pieces within a specific project that are needed to properly describe it.

It's important to work on all three narratives—presentation, visual, project—simultaneously as the design progresses. The presentation design process is not linear, but is really a back and forth design effort between the interrelationships of these three narratives and in the case of a complex design presentation moves forward and backward across an often long design process. It should also be noted that for a design presentation to truly be successful, it is important to work on the presentation from the beginning of the design process. Gone are the days when the designer focuses on just the project design for a certain amount of time and then shifts focus to the design of the presentation. Architectural projects, particularly theoretical ones, are realized only through presentation. You must begin on the presentation the moment you begin on your project design.

To better understand the three types of narratives, let's look at the basic definition of a narrative. A narrative—in the context of presentation design—is a purposeful and composed relationship between elements that are constructed to be understood together.[1]

Presentation Narrative: Goals and Purpose

The presentation narrative is ultimately the order or manner in which the designer wants their project to be revealed during the presentation. This narrative could be manifested through a verbal presentation where the designer essentially verbally "narrates" the design argument using the visual material as a reference to the design ideas that are being verbally described. Or the presentation narrative could be manifested through the order—both through hierarchy relationships and through adjacency relationships—of representational artifacts arranged physically on the presentation boards or in the digital presentation slide deck.

Communication, Representation and Presentation—**The Design Narratives**

This drawing reveals very little about the space of the surface and instead focuses on what spaces are beyond. Unfolded Elevation by Meghan Quigley.

Visual Narrative: Goals and Purpose

Working with the established definition of a narrative and integrating the notion of the visual—all things seen—think of the visual narrative as the deliberate, designed visual relationships between elements in the presentation composed to be understood together and used to clarify the understanding of the project.[2]

Ideas describing the detailed components of a visual narrative are written in subsequent sections of this book. For now, let the following topics give some indication about what types of elements fall under the purview of the visual narrative: grid and alignment systems, visual order, visual hierarchy, typeface usage, etc.

Project Narrative: Goals and Purpose

The project narrative in a presentation relates to the specific project. It is the unique visual and written representational material required to convey the thinking behind the work.[3]

When developing the project narrative for use in a presentation, care should be given to authentically address what you specifically found interesting through the experience of your own design work. It is important to know what should be conveyed about a project. There are many types of normative project components to consider: research, precedent studies, site conditions, basic representational artifacts, etc. It is also important to use the presentation as a place to convey the nature or atmospheric attitude of the project. This can be one of the most interesting parts of designing the project narrative and it ties directly to the visual narrative.

Make sure all of the thinking behind the work is overt; don't leave anything without visual representation and assume it will be obvious to the reviewer. To successfully do this, make a list of all the ideas that need to be conveyed for the project and make sure each of these ideas can be represented with a visual artifact.

Putting the Design Narratives to Work

All three of these design narratives play an important role in the development of your presentation. Keep them all in mind as you move through the process of designing your project. Elements and ideas from each narrative will overlap and blur the lines between the others. Don't worry about this. Design is a messy business; it will ultimately be impossible to keep things in such tidy narrative categories. This means you really are digging in and designing these narratives simultaneously![4]

developing the project narrative

constructing a visual argument

There are many things that go into the development of a compelling design argument; some parts of the argument can start at the beginning of the design project and some things will develop as the design process moves along. Typically, the primary artifacts developed during the course of a design project are visual ones such as drawings, models, images and renderings. Knowing the ideas behind the visual artifacts that are being developed will help hone the representations into meaningful pieces of communication.

There are certain graphic standards that should be understood and implemented by all designers to prevent graphic calamities that can get in the way of clear visual communication. This section aims to help the designer sharpen and integrate both their verbal and visual skills while tackling the challenge of the visual argument.

One of the single most difficult things to achieve with a presentation is a true and powerful visual and verbal representation of design thinking and not just a display of project artifacts. Remember our definition of the project narrative: the project narrative in a presentation relates to the specific project and is the unique visual and written representational material required to convey the design thinking behind the work.

Time is precious during project development and often it is all a designer can do to just get the project visually described. Using design artifacts without thinking about what they are representing is never a good idea when it comes to presentation design. This method of presentation design is just a representation of production. It only demonstrates that artifacts were made, that there is a basic skill set. However, it is missing a radically important skill and, frankly, a more elusive skill to demonstrate: the skill of design thinking.

Often a project reviewer has multiple projects to review. They could even have hundreds of competition submissions to review that they need to narrow down to a short list. Every single project is from a competent designer who has the basic skills of all architecture students—they can build physical models, they can build digital models, and they can all produce a set of drawings. These are skills that are expected! But you are declaring that you are a designer and being a designer requires the demonstration of an inquisitive and robust mind! A designer creates; a designer strives to expose something previously unknown. It is a very specific set of skills to display.

The ultimate challenge in presentation design is to strive to uncover, reveal and explain the design thinking—the previously unknown—through the artifacts of the design project. As a result of successful presentation design, the designer can direct the reviewer to exactly what they want them to see and understand about a project—use this fact to your advantage. Don't simply rely on the material that is available. New visual representations to explain your project may need to be produced in order to explain the complexity of your design ideas.[1]

Finding Gaps in the Project Narrative

It is important to work diligently toward a cohesive and logical project narrative. It is a relatively straightforward process but one that needs to begin early in the project's development.

To get started at the beginning of a project, make a list of the kinds of project representations that should typically exist for a project. This is a list of artifacts that covers the basics: site plan, plans, elevations, sections, descriptive diagrams, etc. As the project progresses, this list will naturally develop and morph depending on the descriptive needs of the project.

Likewise, as the project develops, keep a list of all of the project ideas that are evolving that will ultimately need to be conveyed in the presentation. This list should include every idea that has been incorporated into the project, no matter how significant or insignificant. Do not leave any ideas off this list. As with the artifact representation list, this one will adjust and shift as the project progresses.

The goal with this exercise is to match important ideas to the artifacts that will best describe them. This is your greatest device in the development of both the project and the presentation. So, I will say it again: the goal is to match important ideas to the artifacts that will best describe them.

While moving through the design process, these lists will need to be organized and reordered to establish a hierarchy of design ideas. It is always better to communicate a few ideas and communicate them well than to try to express too much and risk the entire argument becoming unclear, that is why an idea hierarchy is needed. In the case of a presentation, the reviewer spends a relatively short amount of time with the work compared to how long the designer has and it is imperative that the design thinking is clearly conveyed. Prioritizing and acting as a curator to your own design ideas is a must. It is not enough to simply demonstrate your production skills. Design ideas must be represented. If they are not represented in the presentation, they do not exist.

Constructing a Visual Argument—**Developing the Project Narrative**

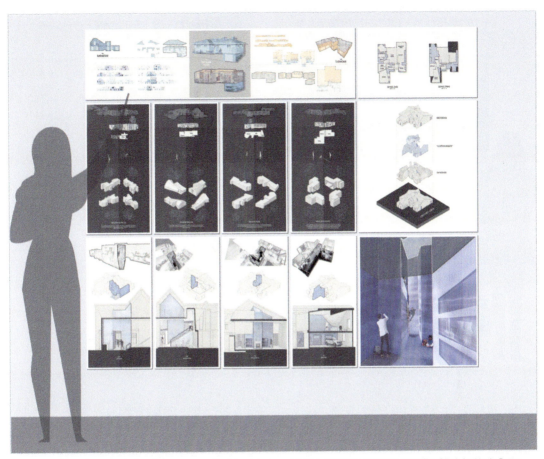

Clear image hierarchy supports the design argument in this printed presentation. Drawing selections from The Glitch by Neely Sutter.

It is entirely likely that additional material of some sort—drawings, models, diagrams—will need to be produced to flesh out your visual argument. It is a critical step in the clarity of your presentation to be realistic with yourself about what needs to be done. It is important to step back and be truly honest with yourself to determine if what you have to show actually delivers the message you intend. If you do decide that additional visual representation is needed, be careful and determine what you can actually accomplish in the time left. If time is limited, be focused and accomplish the work of absolute value to your argument.

Order of the Project Narrative

It is important to give some thoughtful reasoning to the order in which the project is presented. Your first instinct might be to organize the project narrative based on the order in which the project was developed and designed. This could be a reasonable strategy. However, it completely removes any opportunity to build a hierarchical and cohesive design argument. Instead, this method simply describes what you did and in the order you did it. This isn't always the best way to present your work.

Visual Communication for Architects and Designers: constructing the persuasive presentation

Broad categories help organize the complexity of ideas embedded in this thesis presentation, Agro-Pelago: Foodscapes for the Future by Jaclyn Kaloczi.

Try this instead: review the lists generated earlier about project artifacts—existing and missing—and project ideas. From these lists, match design ideas to visual artifacts that best explain them and begin to combine and relate ideas to one another in an effort to streamline your thoughts into similar categories. Through this activity you can establish a hierarchy between the primary ideas and support ideas. Once you understand the hierarchy of ideas, it becomes clearer which representations should appear as the most visually prominent within the presentation—the ones that convey the primary ideas best! Keep in mind that this primary representation could be anything. It could be an exploded axonometric drawing, a plan or a section, a wire-frame sequence of views, a rendered or illustrated perspective view or even an annotated diagram. It could be anything really. The most important thing to remember about the order of the project narrative is that it should be considered and not just a retelling of the history of the development of a project—unless, of course, after careful consideration, you decide this is the best way to present your specific project narrative.

Keep in mind, as the designer you have full control of what the project reviewer understands about the work—absolute and complete control. Take advantage of this knowledge when developing the order of the project narrative. And remember, even though it is good practice to formally structure an argument, there is no way to absolutely control what a reviewer spends time focusing on. They will likely focus on what they, personally, think is the most interesting visual item in the presentation. Making sure to prioritize ideas and their respective representations increases the chance that the focus of the reviewer will go to the place you wish.

Primary Images and Support Images

It is important to establish a strong and pronounced visual hierarchy within the project imagery to determine

Constructing a Visual Argument—**Developing the Project Narrative**

which project representations are most important to the design argument. Once this determination is made, it becomes much easier to make decisions about both the placement of other images as well as their relative size. As mentioned before, images that are most important to the design argument should lead the visual presentation and should be large relative to other artifacts within the presentation. This is a very simple but powerful strategy.

Once the primary images have been identified, it is time to determine which images should act as support images. Primary images are the images that best convey the main design objectives and are generally larger within the presentation. Support images are images that need other visual content to be fully meaningful or images that are purposefully subordinate to a primary image. It is important to understand this relationship between images, to identify the relationships early and to let this information influence the presentation layout.[2]

Begin Constructing Your Presentation

Development of the project and presentation narrative should happen almost simultaneously. In fact, it can be quite difficult to conceptually separate these tasks. This is a good thing! If a presentation is the final outcome of a design project, then the design of the presentation narrative is actually a primary component of the design of the project.

In truth, the evaluation of a design project and therefore the presentation is based on the clarity and conveyance of ideas through the presentation. It is imperative that the presentation demonstrates the designer's ability to think through and solve complex design problems. The presentation is ultimately the only thing being designed for. Your project does not exist anywhere else or in any other way. The presentation is essentially all you have. All drawings you make or models you build are representation tools. Keep this in mind and make sure the design presentation is a clear, compelling and focused message of your design ideas.

systems of visual structure and visual organization

constructing a visual argument

Developing the Visual Narrative

Employing visual structure and visual organization systems across the entire presentation is vital for the visual consistency of the work. In simple terms, without this visual organization, it can be very difficult for reviewers to focus on the design work. The last thing you want to have happen is for reviewers to be so distracted by an inconsistent organization system, that they are completely unable to visually stitch your design argument together. Implementing structured ordering systems is the best way to elevate your presentation from a random set of images on boards to a choreographed collection of work that supports a clear design argument.

There are two important ideals that can be achieved through the consistent application of visual ordering systems:

1. Using visual ordering systems makes it easier for the designer to organize and convey their design ideas. Establishing physical parameters to work within provides constraints to push against—always a good strategy on a design problem and the presentation is certainly a design problem.

2. Having a clear ordering system makes it easier for the reviewer to actually see, follow and understand the design argument.

As you see, simply stated, visual ordering systems work for both the designer and the reviewer and exist as a primary means through which a message can be effectively delivered.

Fortunately, there is a full collection of systems that can be used to attain visual organization—grid and alignment systems, hanglines and baselines, the active area and margins, adjacency relationships—and all can operate together as both visual organization systems and content organization systems. These systems work in conjunction with each other to achieve the visual structure needed to consistently organize a presentation—this describes the nature of the visual narrative.

Grid and Alignment Systems

There are several different visual structures and visual organization systems that are important to understand when developing presentation strategies. The primary and most relevant organizational system is a physical structure called a grid and alignment system. This system alone does the most work toward visually organizing graphic content and supporting the design argument. All other systems work in a conjunctive manner to the grid and alignment system. These other systems pertain specifically to how images and text relate to one another visually, and how these images and text relate to the page (board, slide, etc.). Ultimately grid and alignment systems are the primary tool for arranging material on the presentation board.

Typically for board layout, a combination of both alignment systems and grid systems is required. Grid and alignment systems can be challenging. However, it is possible to have a successful underlying structural system without letting the system get too unwieldy and frustrating. If you strive to understand the fundamental principles of both a grid and alignment system and commit to following and implementing this structural system within the presentation, your presentation will be ordered successfully. Most grid systems are relatively flexible and it's easy to combine several grid systems together to create additional flexibility to the structure. Keep in mind, baselines, hanglines and simple alignments and adjacency groupings are incredibly helpful when laying out boards.

There are many different types of grid systems that designers use for page layout, like you might do in your portfolio. These grid systems typically fall into the following categories: single column grid, multi-column grids—this could be two, three, four, etc. columns—and the modular or compound grid. For the purposes of a presentation, whether in board layout or digital layout, a modular or compound grid is typically the most clear way to move forward.

Margins, hanglines, baselines, the actual grid, defined spatial zones and grid modules are the basic elements of a simple grid system. All of these elements exist in each different size grid or alignment system; the only difference is the change in the proportion of the relationships within each system. Spatial zones are determined through the aggregation of individual grid modules by combining adjacent cells. Combining modules together to establish different spatial zones within a grid system will generate a very flexible modular grid. Paying attention to simple edge alignments across the entire grid system also creates needed flexibility within the system. When making these adjustments to the grid, be cautious and make sure that the grid is not completely undermined. Applying too many adjustments could potentially remove the legibility of the grid all together.

Ultimately the primary goal of using a grid or alignment system is to provide an underlying structure to help visually organize graphic content. Be careful not to let the content get overrun by the structure of the grid. If that starts to happen, it's time to break the grid and adjust the layout visually and intuitively as needed. Usually, simple edge alignments can be very helpful to resolve these issues.

Modular or Compound Grid

A modular or compound grid system combines horizontal rows and vertical columns into a grid system. The resultant orthogonal grid creates modules that can be combined in a horizontal or vertical direction. This type of grid is incredibly flexible and is an easy choice for the wide range of content types found within a design presentation.

Alignment Systems Within the Grid

The most important thing to understand about any grid structure for a presentation is how to modify the grid for a flexible arrangement of material. All grid systems can merge grid cells together to create super-cells that still adhere to the original grid structure. Fundamentally, grids consist of alignment relationships more than anything else and can be incredibly flexible if they are thought of as systems to maintain edge alignments rather than boxes that need to be filled with visual content.[3]

It is important to remember that items placed in adjacent relationships within a system will be read as a set of information. Align certain elements such that they

Constructing a Visual Argument—**Systems of Visual Structure and Visual Organization**

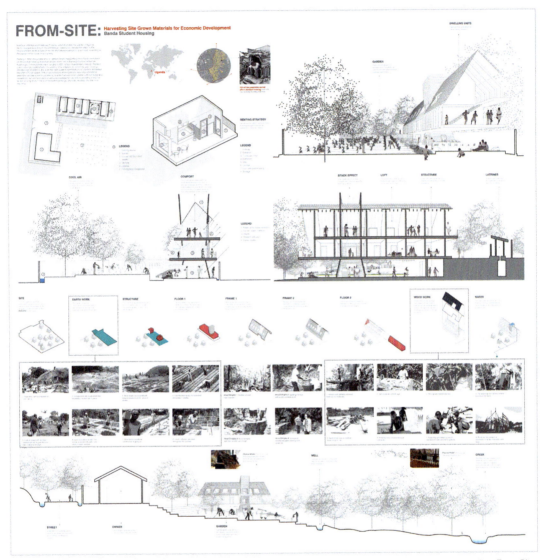

Organizing similar content in sub-zones and relating content from one zone to the next adds visual clarity to this presentation, From-Site: Banda Student Housing, Harvesting Site Grown Materials for Economic Development by Joel Jassu.

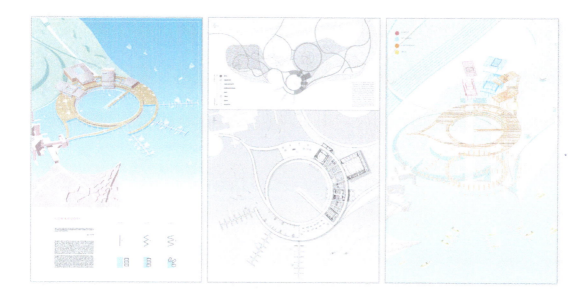

are purposefully read together as a set. To do this you will need to adjust internal margins of the set so that the items in the set are closer together than the margins provided by the grid. When set up in this manner, this grouping of material will read as one unit within the entire grid system.

Hanglines, Baselines and Vertical Alignments as Organizing Elements

Hanglines and baselines are implied horizontal lines that extend across zones in the presentation and act as organizing elements. Content hangs from the hangline and sits on the baseline. It is entirely possible to have a compound grid that uses hanglines and baselines as a primary means to arrange content across various boards and establishes alignment relationships not directly found within the grid system. This will happen in instances where content doesn't quite fit the proportion of the compound grid. In this case, pull hanglines or baselines from other areas of the presentation to make a secondary set of systematic alignments. Vertical alignments work in the same manner as horizontal hanglines and baselines by providing a vertical edge for alignment. Vertical alignments tend to establish columnar relationships while hanglines and baselines tend to establish horizontal or row relationships. Be sure to establish a primary alignment orientation for the reading of your presentation—horizontal or vertical—and use the other as a secondary direction. This will help the reviewer understand how to spatially move through the content within the presentation.

Occasionally, content just does not work with all of the visual rules that have been established for a presentation. The bottom line is this: if the layout looks strange to the point that it is visually distracting to the legibility of the content, change the layout. Often there is content that needs to rely on optical correctness so that it simply "looks" correct. In these cases, rely on the designer's eye to correct the visual distractions. Just be careful not to stray too far away from the system. An entirely new visual distraction could be developed!

Getting Started

When beginning your presentation layout, it can be hard to know exactly which grid or alignment system to use. It

Constructing a Visual Argument—**Systems of Visual Structure and Visual Organization**

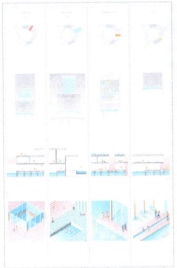

This set of boards relies on a system of organization for each board while the overall color scheme and elegant nature of the drawings visually stitches them together. Flow & Fluidity by Annika Babra.

may be easier to begin by thinking about the hierarchical structure of the design argument and the pieces of visual representation that explain those ideas. Grouping similar content—either visually similar or of similar idea type—might also help establish an initial system of organization. Being familiar with the content available for the presentation as you are beginning to design the underlying structural system is helpful.

In reality, it is entirely possible that there is a mix of multiple systems. As you progress through the design process and begin to get the design argument structured, the visual argument will follow. Patterns will emerge as the layouts progress that will lend themselves to certain structural systems. Some designers begin the layouts with a certain system in mind and then let things morph as actual content is added. Be aware that sometimes it will come time to completely abandon a grid or alignment system that isn't working and simply try something new.

There is a certain look and feel to all well-designed presentations that can be elusive to the designer without an understanding of underlying grid and alignment

systems. Make sure your presentation doesn't feel unorganized because there isn't a strong point of view when it comes to the layout design.

A Note on Text and Column Width

Keep the guidelines in mind for the character maximums and minimums in a line of text when employing your grid system. Characters in a column of text should fall somewhere within the 45–75 characters per line range. When a line of characters is significantly shorter than that range, the text can become more difficult to read because the content is visually choppy. When a line of characters is longer than that range, the distance for the eye to travel from the end of a line of text to the beginning of the next line of text is so long that the reader can easily get lost. Both extremes lead to legibility issues and significantly reduce the comprehension of your text content. It's not an exact science, however, so get close to the suggested range but depending on typeface size and style you can stray a little from the recommendation.

Visual Communication for Architects and Designers: constructing the persuasive presentation

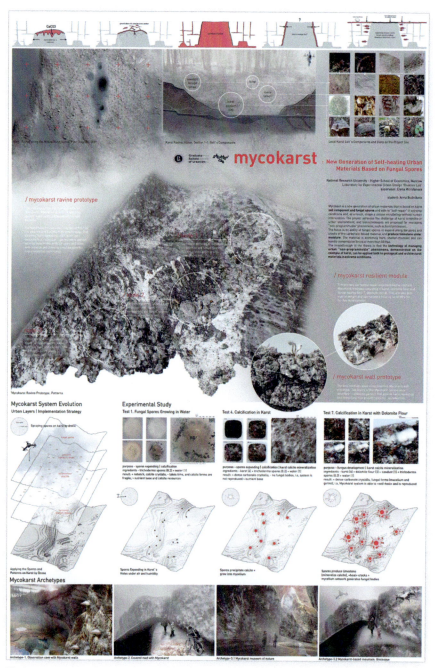

The large, central image directs the eye to the primary content; ordered sub-sets organize the remaining visual content in this presentation, Mycokarst: New Generation of Self-Healing Urban Materials Based on Fungal Spores by Anna Budnikova.

Constructing a Visual Argument—**Systems of Visual Structure and Visual Organization**

Strong horizontal alignments organize much of this board presentation. However, vertical arrangements, as can been seen at the upper right, create a secondary alignment system. Gateway at Raccoon Creek by Matthew Williams.

Designing the Layout: Active Area and Margins

The active area of a layout—or live area as it is often called—is basically the area of the layout that is available to place visual material. Designing the active area is an important step in the visual organization of a presentation. It helps different graphic material read as if it all belongs cohesively together.

The active area in a presentation is typically different than how you might think of the active area in a publication such as your portfolio. In a publication the active area is defined by the margins established on the pages and includes the folio matter—header and footer material—as well as the primary hanglines and baselines. In a presentation, it is a little different. Particularly on board layouts, the main thing to consider is maintaining consistent margin relationships between the presentation content and the edge of the boards. It is quite simple to do this but don't write it off as something not worth setting up. Establish the edge margins of your boards paying particular attention to what happens at the edges where multiple boards abut; you don't want a double margin to appear. Make sure that multiple boards, or slides, within a single presentation respond to the same active area; this is an important step in designing the cohesive nature of an entire presentation.

Margins

A well-designed set of margins clearly defines the active area and is consistently used board after board or slide after slide. These margins provide enough white space on the page to firmly root the visual material to the page. A poorly designed set of margins either has too much white space around the visual material or not enough white space. Too much white space makes the images feel compressed as if the white space has too much visual power over the images—it becomes difficult to visually enter the material. Too little white space makes the images feel as if they are sliding off the page and can make the images so uncomfortable on the page that it is again difficult to visually enter them.[4] There are a few very simple rules to follow that will make the design of the layout margins simple and successful. Just remember that setting up the margins is ultimately purposefully designing the active area. Typically, when setting up margins for any layout, the bottom margin is slightly larger than the side and top margins. This is particularly important when there is only one image on a page or board. With multi-image presentation layouts, keep this in mind as well. The bottom of the layout page has to respond to issues of optical weight and the visual gravity of the page. Just as objects in three-dimensional space have a relationship to gravity, so too do visual objects on a page. Simply put, if the bottom margin is at the same distance as the other outside margins, objects will appear to fall off the bottom of the page. By increasing the bottom margin slightly, it gives adequate white space to balance the visual tendency for graphic material to slide uncomfortably down to the bottom of the page. Of course, there are also plenty of ways to design the presentation with no margins at all! See the sections on image bleeds and visual weight for additional ideas.

When to Break the Rules

There are always instances where the rules defined in the visual narrative of a presentation must be broken just to maintain visual legibility.

Optical Edges and Margins
One way to break the rules relative to margins and the active area of a layout is by passing graphic material beyond the optical edge of a margin. Small pieces of drawings, titles or, in some cases, punctuation can extend into the board margin as long as the primary visual material stays within the optical edge. Determining what can extend beyond the optical edge depends largely on the visual weight of the piece considered for extension. Extending a visually heavy graphic beyond the optical edge will effectively shorten the margin. Therefore, only extend those items beyond the optical edge that are visually lighter than other objects on the board. This will visually maintain the proper margins while allowing for some flexibility right at the optical edge.[5] You can determine the success or failure of this extension by stepping back and squinting at the boards. Make sure the margins are primarily

Constructing a Visual Argument—**Systems of Visual Structure and Visual Organization**

Framing a perspective view by extending planes into three-dimensional space visually enlarges the perception of space. Drawing selection from Carve & Construct by Mert Kansu.

maintained even though small amounts of content have pushed past them.

There is also an opportunity to break the optical edge of margins within the grid system; it is not only an option for the condition at the edge of the board. Often, breaking the optical edge—usually a rectangle in an architectural presentation—will increase the legibility of a particular image by breaking the edge with a perspective line. This perspective line extends into the space of the reviewer and literally draws them physically into the image.

One note of caution when extending perspective lines beyond the frame of the image: be careful to align any text—typically a caption—with the actual edge of the perspective line and not the edge of the image frame in Adobe InDesign. Captions need to visually belong to the image they are supporting.

Using Bleeds to Direct the Eye

Image bleeds are another effective way to bend the rules that define the active area of a layout. A bleed is an image that essentially bleeds to the edge of the page, extending past margins to the edge of the layout. There are several types of bleeds:

1. Full bleed: A full bleed is where the image bleeds over all four edges of a layout, erasing any margins that have been established.

Visual Communication for Architects and Designers: constructing the persuasive presentation

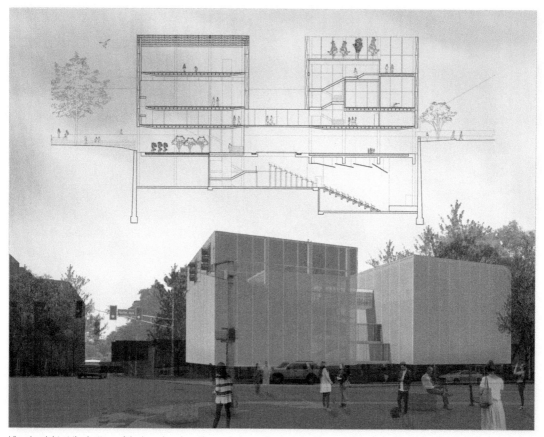

Visual weight at the bottom of the board anchors the rendering on the board while providing space for the section, line drawing to float on a separate layer above. Drawing selection from Stage of the Art, Light Gallery by Maria Pastorelli, Clay Kiningham and Julie Pierides.

2. Partial bleed: A partial bleed obliterates the margin in one to three of the edges of a layout. So at least one edge still maintains the proper, established margin.

In a presentation, use bleeds to draw the eye to specific content. Any time that the established system is broken—such as bleeds or altered optical edges—the eye of the reviewer will be drawn to that specific element. Use this to your advantage when designing your presentation layout.

Keep in mind, particularly in board layout design, because of issues of optical weight, the designer will often place a visually heavy object at the bottom of the board. This is fine, and often at the bottom of the board, margins are ignored completely and a full bleed is used. A great example of this is placing a section drawing at the bottom of the layout and letting the poché of the ground extend as a full bleed across the bottom of the page.[6]

Constructing a Visual Argument—**Systems of Visual Structure and Visual Organization**

In this four board design presentation, notice the visual weight of the section poché to effectively anchor the drawing to the board. Acclimate by Cameron Foster and Phil Riazzi.

Visual Communication for Architects and Designers: constructing the persuasive presentation

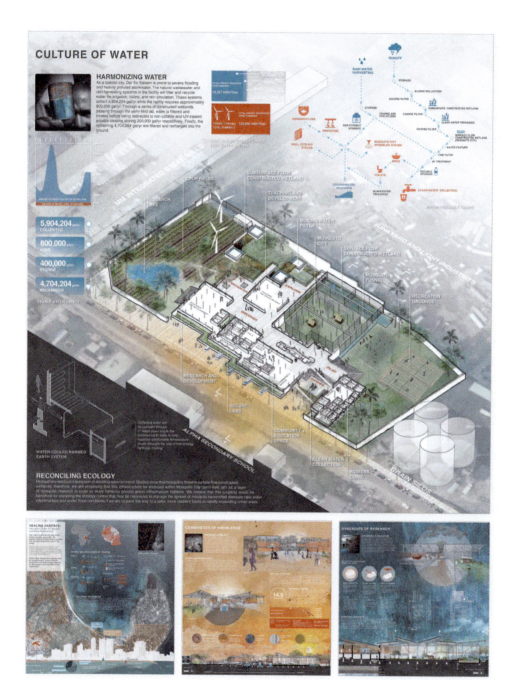

The large primary image is used to convey design, programmatic and organizational information. The bands of color along the three lower boards anchor each board individually and tie these boards together. Healing Habitats: Innovation Center for Disease and Water Management by Natalia Sabrina Ortiz Luna, Elena Koepp and Catherine Earley.

Visual Relationship Between Objects on a Page

The nature of the adjacency relationships between objects on a page can radically alter the reading of content. These relationships are defined by each object's relative proximity to the next. Every visual item within the layout has a margin around it that determines its specific relationship to the next object. Objects that have smaller margins—than other margins on the layout—between them will be read as pairs or sets of objects and therefore will be understood together as a conceptual unit.

Bottom line, working to adjust margins to reflect the relationships between objects on a page will help organize the visual content and thus the legibility of the design argument. It is one of the single most important things you can do to visually structure your design argument.

Visually Entering the Content

The manner in which visual information is arranged on a layout directly affects a person's ability to visually enter the content within the presentation. But what does that mean exactly—visually enter the content? The clearest definition is to think of it as a person's ability to quickly understand the message of each representation. Your design goal is to make sure each piece of content is comprehended by the reviewer. It is not enough to just include visual material on a layout; it must be ordered in a way that makes it visually digestible. There are two basic ways a person can view a presentation layout:

1. The reviewer can see the pattern that is established through the grid and adjacencies that are employed OR

2. The reviewer can see past the organizational grid system and visually enter an image and immediately comprehend the intent of the content.

Obviously, it is preferred to have a project reviewer understand the message behind the visual representations rather than just view the presentation at a surface level, only seeing the pattern of the arrangement of images. Ultimately, the message behind the design work—the design thinking—should be retained by the reviewer—an image or series of images that they will relate back to the design argument. It would be a significant loss if all they remembered were the patterns of image alignments and not the message behind the work.

Making appropriate arrangements and alignments so that the content is understood is one of the primary challenges for a visual presentation to be successful. There are several approaches to achieve this and it is usually a combination of them all that works best.

Visual Stickiness: The Power of the Primary Image

Visual stickiness is the idea that an image or series of images is so visually powerful that it only takes one glance for that particular image to be remembered.[7] An image's stickiness relates to its ability to be recalled mentally. Keep the idea of visual stickiness in mind when designing your presentation and think through your project representations and design a primary image that conveys a large and important amount of your fundamental design ideas. This image should be large and visually powerful relative to other content in the presentation. This primary and visually sticky image could be any type of drawing, diagram or image as long as it is visually compelling and conveys the primary message of the project.

It would be ideal for a presentation reviewer to be able to recall specific content long after reviewing the work. In fact, this would be really necessary for a competition review! The reviewer has potentially hundreds of submissions to review. You want yours remembered!

Visual Legibility and Size of Images

Another way to think about the visual hierarchy of images is by determining image size based on image legibility. Basically, this means you can decide how big or small an image needs to be within the layout based on whether or not an image is acceptably legible at a smaller size or if it really needs to be larger to allow the reviewer to understand the image. Use a ranking system as follows:

1. Image needs to be full scale (very large) to be legible.
2. Image needs to be half scale to be legible.
3. Image is legible as a thumbnail.[8]

This simple system can help you sort through your images and make an initial determination about image size solely based on scalar image legibility. You may find that images that you have not spent enough time on must be smaller to look resolved and vice versa. However, it is important that legibility by size aligns with size needs based on the delivery of the argument. For instance, a rendered image that is very important to the design argument with only schematic design resolution will actually look more powerful if presented at a smaller scale and perhaps in a series of multiple views. Nonetheless, if it is really important to the design argument and therefore needs to be larger on the boards, you've identified some work that needs to be completed.

The opposite design resolution scenario is also tricky. A rendering that has been resolved down to every minuscule detail can look unclear or visually cluttered when reduced to a very small size when put in the presentation.

Bottom line, check to make sure the visual representations you develop are resolved to the size they will need to be within the presentation to support the design argument. This can work to your advantage by helping you focus your energy where it is needed. An underdeveloped rendering can look great at 3" x 5" and absolutely hideous and undesigned when shown at 9" x 15". It all has to do with the design resolution of the proposed image. Again, put your design energy into resolving those representations that need to be larger in the presentation to explain primary design ideas.

Adjacency Relationships

We've already briefly discussed the advantages of making slight spacing adjustments between visual content to vary the reading and understanding of graphic material by assembling material into adjacent content sets. In presentation design, this simple ordering principle can be used in a purposeful way to help make sense of scads of content that is needed to make a complex visual argument. In general, visual content located within a close adjacency relationship will be understood as a grouping or set of information and can be read with the same content definition. However, it is important to understand how to use these adjacency relationships to your advantage and to understand the ramifications of each adjacency decision.

Content Pairs
Content pairs function as a set of two objects. The adjacency relationship should allow the two elements to visually attach to one another and for the pair to separate from the other content on the layout. This pairing is achieved through the reduction of the margin between the objects relative to other margins in the layout. Content pairs can have either a vertical or horizontal relationship. A pairing of images is particularly effective when setting up comparisons—this versus that or this and that.

Content Sets
Content sets behave similarly to content pairs but with more content elements in play. The adjacency relationships between all elements in a content set must be exactly the same such that the entire set reads as a whole. In other words, the margins between objects in a content set must all be the same and should be smaller than other margins on the layout in order for them to be read and understood together. Content sets can have solely vertical relationships, solely horizontal relationships or a combination of vertical and horizontal relationships in more of a grid arrangement.

Content Series
Content series are a little trickier to define. They operate similarly to pairs and sets regarding the spacing in between objects. The margins between objects in a content series must all be the same and should be smaller than other margins on the layout in order for them to be read and understood together. The primary difference for a content series is that the series is trying to visually describe a transformation of content across the series. In this type of visual set, the content needs to be visually similar enough such that the reader can determine the differences between each piece

of content in the series. It is a tight balance between similarity and difference. An easy way to achieve a content series is to start with a similar base—as in a diagram—and adjust just enough of the base in each step to convey difference.

Chronology Content
Chronology content displays content in the order in which it was generated. While chronology content is relative to time in the sense of order, the chronology is not tied to specific periods of time.

Timeline Content
Timeline content is similar to chronology content. However, timeline content is tied to specific intervals of time. Drawings expressing the passage of time are even more difficult to represent and tend to fall into a category called drawing as narrative.

Video and Film Content
Video and film content provides specific challenges when included in a presentation format that does not allow for the video to be played as originally designed. However, it can be quite effective in a presentation to display film stills in a linear and adjacent relationship. While it's not possible to show an entire film in a print format, it is possible to convey the visual quality of the film and the gist of its content. It won't be the same but the film can take on a new and different existence in print. Film stills should be gathered making selections based on visual importance and arranged in a linear fashion so that they are read in a continuous fashion—just as films are understood—with no visual gaps between the images. Shifting each row of content right or left so that there are no vertical margin alignments between film rows will help with the horizontal reading of the film. Also, let the images bleed off the page both right and left to imply movement—this also aids in the visual understanding of the stills in a cinematic relationship.

Four Square Grids
Four square grids are a common ordering system that should be avoided. When content is arranged in a four square grid, the most powerful visual element is the white space void at the intersection of the grid. Naturally the eye goes automatically to the center point of the grid and, therefore, the meaning of the content is visually lost. There are a variety of ways to break a four square grid just through hierarchy assignments. In a typical four square grid all four images have the exact same visual weight. Assigning hierarchy—and therefore difference in size—to the four images will automatically shift the void caused by the margins out of the center thus eliminating the visual problem.

A Note on Caption and Drawing and Diagram Title Adjacencies
Captions and titles require special care when they are placed within the layout of a presentation. Captions and titles—in this case things like diagram or drawing titles—must visually attach to those items they are captioning or titling. If these elements don't visually attach and instead are too far away from their respective content, they will read as a separate and distinct visual object on the page. This will visually clutter the layout and bring too much attention to the caption or title. If they are properly attached to their respective content and have employed appropriate hierarchy as a support item, they will support the visual content instead of distracting from it. Basically, without proper adjacency to the content they support, captions and titles become extra visual elements cluttering the page.

White Space on Page
White space on a page is exactly as it sounds—empty areas that have no content. Be aware that white space isn't necessarily white. It is simply the absence of content. You could equate white space to blank space. However, white space is fundamentally different than blank space. White space is the designed areas that lack content. Blank space is often considered to be leftover space. There is a significant difference. Challenge the desire to fill an entire layout densely with imagery; it is one of the biggest mistakes made in presentation design. There are instances when dense image series or sets on a presentation layout make sense but following specific adjacency rules for series or sets will help minimize visual over-density.

Visual Communication for Architects and Designers: constructing the persuasive presentation

above and right: Primary images organize content on each board while color families and similar graphic sensibilities tie the boards together. Nurture: Lehigh Living Cultural Center by Kurt Kimsey and Matthew Wieber.

Constructing a Visual Argument—Systems of Visual Structure and Visual Organization

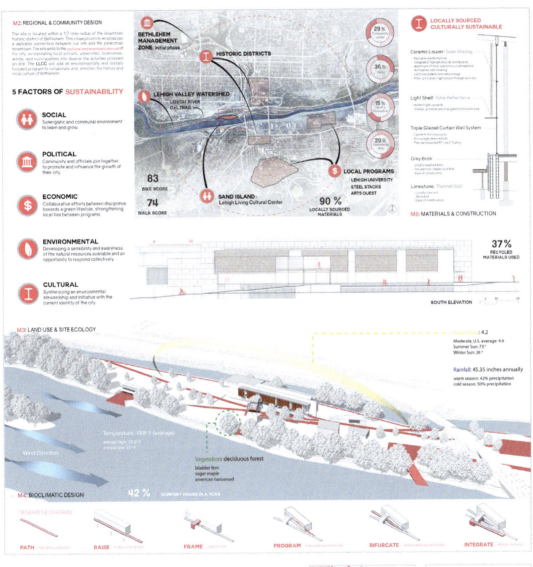

Visual Communication for Architects and Designers: constructing the persuasive presentation

Adequate white space on a page provides directionality for the eye to move around the page by creating different zones of visual rest to move through before reading the next area of visual content. This strategy allows for visual breathing room so the eye can enter content and retreat from content. All of this visual movement happens subconsciously, but without the necessary designed white space the eye begins to read the pattern of the layout instead of the content.

If the layout uses completely equal white space on all sides of the images, the content will appear fixed as if the static white space is visually containing the content. This makes it difficult for the eye to move around the page and actually "enter" or "see" the content of the visual material. Varying the white space zones creates a more dynamic layout and encourages the eye to move quickly in some areas and linger in others.

Keep in mind, neither varied nor equal white space is necessarily better, they are just different and it is important to understand the difference.

Overlapping Content
As a general rule, overlapping content is visually distracting and should be approached with caution. Simply overlapping one image with another confuses hierarchy relationships by cluttering two objects on one layer creating a compound object—it basically takes on the shape of the two objects conflated on top of one another. Overlapping images as a graphic strategy should be completely avoided. However, there are some interesting exceptions to this rule. Overlapping images like you might have done for a family scrapbook is a complete no-no. But using the idea to purposefully create a hierarchical order by establishing a foreground, middle ground and background could be an interesting way to visually separate content on the layout. For this to be legible, you must use graphic strategies to objectify visual content on the top layer while being aware that content left to the background will appear specifically flat with the objectified content on top.

In addition, only overlap content that either creates a multiplicity of information or connects one section of content with another. Never overlap two pieces of complex representations, this will create visual confusion. Only overlay one image over another when it is designed purposefully. It is better to think of this as an encroachment and not an overlap.

Overlapping image with text is another possibility that should be approached with discretionary caution. Often, there are situations where by necessity text must overlap an image. In these instances, be careful that there isn't so much text over an image that either the text becomes illegible or the image becomes illegible.

The biggest challenge when placing text over an image is that if the image has a variety of values, there could be places where the text is legible but other places where the text blends in with the tones in the image. A potential solution is to create a transparent film—a block of transparent color—between the text and the image to create a middle ground that helps neutralize any areas where the text and image may begin to blend together. Experiment with this system because each instance with different text and a different image and a different transparent color film will all create different outcomes.

There is one last situation to consider. Images—usually drawings—with pure white backgrounds can overlap in the Adobe InDesign file but still not read as if they are visually overlapping because the overlap happens in the white area. In this instance, they are technically overlapping but it isn't legible in the final layout because the actual overlap disappears into the white of the page and is not read as an overlap at all.[9]

When Content Jumps a Board
Often when you have a presentation made up of multiple boards, content might get split over multiple boards. It is best practice to avoid this situation. However, in some instances, multiple boards must be used simply because material cannot be printed in such large sheets. In this case, design the board as if it were the full size of all boards placed together and try to be smart about what content jumps across the internal edges. Avoid splitting a specifically detailed drawing or image; it will show up after printing due to the difficulty in getting things to align properly. It is also very difficult to get printed alignments

Constructing a Visual Argument—**Systems of Visual Structure and Visual Organization**

Foreground, middle ground and background layers are used to separate multiple levels of content. Also note white space does not have to be white! Liminal Moments: Chapel + Archeology Museum by Henry Savoie.

correct if visual content jumps the boards at a four board, center corner alignment. Try to avoid this.

Basics of Visual Order and Visual Hierarchy
Visual order and visual hierarchy are two ordering principles that achieve similar goals through different means. Visual order refers to the legibility and understanding of ideas as presented in a specific visual arrangement, grouping or order. Visual hierarchy is an ordering principle defined by relative importance as described through relative size. Both principles work toward a similar goal of visual organization. They are both powerful structural systems to utilize when laying out your materials. Detailed information on these principles can be found in the section titled Basics of Graphic Design as Related to Presentation Design.

Visual Communication for Architects and Designers: constructing the persuasive presentation

Constructing a Visual Argument—**Systems of Visual Structure and Visual Organization**

While not the same experience as the film in its original form, it is possible to use a film if only a printed presentation is permitted. Follow the guidelines in this section to maximize this cinematic presentation. Film title, The Paradox, by Je Sung Lee.

basics of graphic design as related to presentations

constructing a visual argument

Basic principles of graphic design are important for visual clarity and since one of our primary goals in presentation design is visual clarity, it stands to reason we should learn these. There are quite a few fundamentals that can be gleaned from the profession of graphic design and used as guidance for our objectives in presentation design. This section covers graphic issues that are most relevant for our purposes. For additional information on how principles of graphic design can further impact your design work, there are many good texts available. Keep in mind, however, that graphic design is a completely different design profession with issues unique to its own goals and objectives. For architects, all principles of graphic design should be read through an architectural lens. The same rule applies for other design professions that lie outside of graphic design.

Visual Order and Visual Hierarchy

It is difficult to separate the concepts of visual order and visual hierarchy; they are indeed closely related. Both visual order and visual hierarchy work toward visual clarity within a presentation and are applicable for all presentation types. There can be quite a bit of overlap when working with these two principles; just keep in mind that they both are working to help the designer make visual sense of all of the different constituent parts of a design argument.

Visual order describes the visual cohesiveness of objects ordered together to create a united design argument. In general, remember, the visual goal is for a presentation to read as an ordered set of visual information. There could be an instance where visual discordance works for emphasis, but this situation should be the anomaly to the rule of cohesive order.

Remember, visual hierarchy and visual order are very closely related. To think of them differently consider this: visual order relies on the grouping and organization of visual material to establish order while visual hierarchy relies on relative size or weight to establish order. Correctly applied strategies of visual hierarchy strengthen the visual order and vice versa. Keep in mind, to create visual hierarchy, objects on the page must recede visually in order for other visual objects to come forward; this will automatically establish a visual order.

To simplify: visual order helps with the legibility of your graphics. Visual hierarchy is one of the primary tools used to establish visual order.[10]

Many different components of a design presentation are discussed in this publication. Principles of visual hierarchy and visual order are innately ingrained in these discussions. In fact, most of the organizational strategies found throughout this book are describing the complexity of systems that create visual order through visual hierarchy. Pay attention and implement typeface relationships through hierarchy, image adjacency through hierarchy, the hierarchical relationship of content to the board, the three levels of reading of a physical presentation, and the list goes on. Suffice it to say, all issues related to graphic layout have visual hierarchy and visual order as a foundation.

Visual Order: Physical Board Presentations versus Digital Presentations

Keep in mind when you are working on a physical presentation such as a competition entry or simple board presentation, that all elements of the presentation are visible at one time and it is imperative that the entire presentation is designed in a way that follows appropriate visual order and visual hierarchy for all of the visual elements in your presentation. It is a significant amount of visual information to organize so that your communication goals are achieved. Your primary goal is to make sure your complex ideas are visually understandable and in line with your design argument.

A digital presentation is a little different in that often you will not have all of the visual information visible at the same time. In this scenario it is important to make sure the design goal of each slide is clearly understood. Apply principles of visual order and visual hierarchy appropriately so that it reads on each individual slide as well as continuously across all slides.

There are several principles to discuss relative to visual order; keep in mind the goal of visual cohesion and order on both your board layouts and digital presentations with each one.

Hierarchical Communication of Design Ideas: Location of Primary Images

We have already established in earlier sections of this book the need to tie design ideas to design artifacts. We have also described a process through which the designer can establish project ideas and put them in a hierarchical order. It stands to reason then, that this hierarchical list of ideas should be tied to images that will in turn become prominent parts of the visual argument. These images are called primary images and should be designed to be the most important to the design message being delivered. These images need careful consideration regarding size and placement within the presentation.

Constructing a Visual Argument—**Basics of Graphic Design as Related to Presentations**

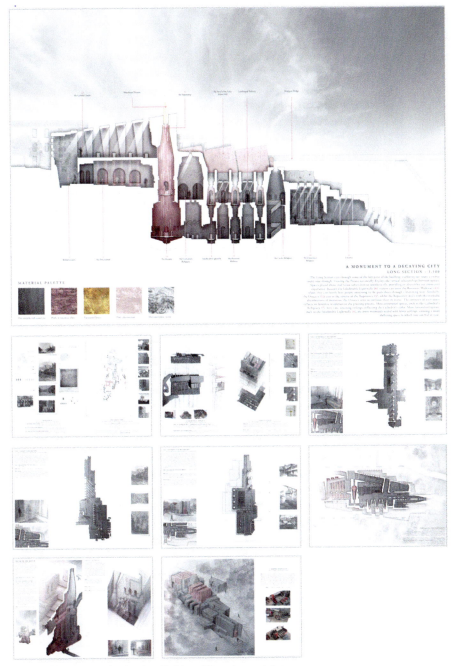

Complex ideas are seamlessly ordered in this multi-board presentation. Color families, primary versus secondary images and appropriate typeface hierarchy all work together to support the graphic dissemination of ideas. Melaphyre: A Monument to a Decaying City by George Newton with Mani Lall.

45

Visual Communication for Architects and Designers: constructing the persuasive presentation

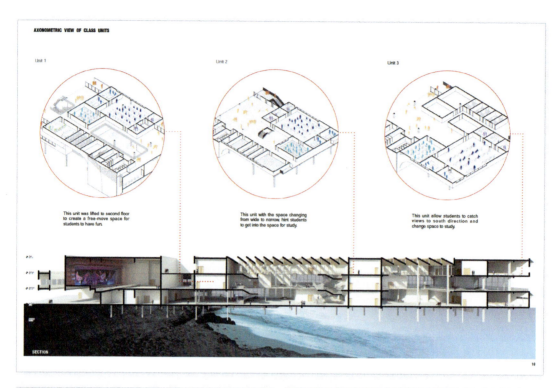

The primary section drawing is used to order the secondary unit axonometric views. The two drawing types work together to explain complex spatial relationships. Sailing: Middle School Design in Galveston, Texas by Wei Lin.

It is important to allow the primary image(s) to be significantly larger than other visual material within the presentation so they emerge as meaningful to the visual argument. If all of the visual content is the same size and therefore the same visual weight, it will be very confusing for the reviewer to determine where to focus their eyes to begin to understand the design argument. The hierarchy established through the use of primary images will make the boards easier to view and easier to comprehend.

Also, keep in mind that there are many different types of images and/or drawings that could be the primary image. The primary image does not always need to be a fully rendered photo-realistic three-dimensional version of your design proposal. The primary image could be a model photo, a plan diagram, an idea diagram, a sketch, an axonometric, a series of images, anything really, as long as it is the image that does the best job of a holistic representation of your project's primary design ideas. If a reviewer can look at the primary image in your presentation and get a sense of the intentions of your project and the ideas behind it, you've selected the correct primary image and it is doing its job!

Images versus Text

Images and text often visually compete with one another in a presentation layout, particularly if an appropriate visual hierarchy hasn't been determined. On the board layout, establish which elements should be the most visually prominent. This decision depends on the component of the project narrative that is most important to convey. Throughout your presentation identify when images should be primary and text secondary and vice versa. The typical relationship should be images as primary visual objects with text used as visual support. For this hierarchical relationship to be visually correct, make sure that when you look at the image, all you see is the image and then you have the opportunity to move your eyes to the supportive text. If, when you look at the image, your eyes are jumping between the text and image, it is likely that your hierarchical relationship between the image and the text is incorrect. Either make the text smaller or the image larger. In either case, correct the hierarchy error.

The size of the title of the entire presentation is one of the few places that a typical hierarchical relationship between image and text can be inverted. In physical presentations where boards are required, the title should be visually legible from at least 5 feet (1.5 meters) from the wall. The size of the text for the title should rise above any other piece of text in the presentation; this will herald it as the title of the board. The title could stand alone or be integrated and overlapped with the primary image. Note: this is one of the few instances where overlapping is an acceptable graphic idea. The title of your presentation is a fantastic opportunity to tell reviewers what the primary design objectives of your project are. It is important to get this right!

How to Use White Space to Establish Appropriate Adjacencies

The proper use of white space within a presentation can be a powerful tool to establish visual order. In this case white space can be used as a tool to help understand which elements on a board belong to one another. By grouping relevant information together, use white space to establish groups as visual packs of information that together deliver a message about your project. As an example, for a set of images to read as a group, make the white space (margins) between the objects smaller than other areas of white space (margins) within the layout. The close adjacency relationship between elements within the groupings rely on white space on the board to recognize appropriate separations and adjacencies between all objects on the board.

Visual Weight

A very simple description of visual weight is defined as an object's ability to attract the eye within a graphic layout. Visual weight can help visual order and lend clarity to a visual argument by drawing the eye toward the primary content. Visual weight can also act as a deterrent and draw the eye to a visual distraction within the presentation. While developing your presentation, always take time to step back, squint and see if your eye is drawn to your primary image(s) or if it is being erroneously drawn to something that you don't intend.

Visual gravity at the bottom of this drawing anchors the variety of descriptive elements found within the layout. Risk Topographies by Alberto de Salvatierra, Chella Strong and Gege Wang.

Visual Communication for Architects and Designers: constructing the persuasive presentation

Remember, visual gravity doesn't have to be dark, white works as well as demonstrated in this section drawing. Cherry County Artists' Hub by Sahr Qureishi.

Relationship to Visual Gravity

Another way to look at the issue of visual weight as it relates to design presentations is the perceived relationship between the reviewer and gravity. This perceived relationship is called visual gravity. Visual gravity is similar to visual weight and has to do with elements that draw the eye but in the case of visual gravity, these objects tend to be anchored at the bottom of the page. In this case, our relationship to the three-dimensional world translates to our relationship to the two-dimensional world primarily through our visual understanding of gravity.

For the purposes of this discussion, consider gravity as the force that attracts us to any other physical body of mass—the force that attracts the body to the center of the earth. Now consider the two-dimensional visual representation of the expression of gravity with the visual weight located at the bottom of the board. In this sense, collecting visually heavy material at the bottom of a layout will visually ground the entire page. There could be instances where it is important to have these visually heavy objects in a location on the board that is not on the bottom. This is perfectly fine! However, be aware that some visual balance issues may need to resolved such that the board doesn't appear top heavy and without appropriate visual order. It is easier for humans to feel that visual weight at the bottom of a board is more balanced than visual weight at the top of a board just due to the aforementioned visual relationship to gravity. It's not a problem, just something to be aware of so that appropriate visual balance can be employed.

Color in the Presentation

The use of color is a powerful tool in establishing or devolving order within a presentation. It is important to understand all of the opportunities and pitfalls of color so that you can be in control of the variety of hierarchy challenges the use of color affords. This section aims to describe a series of different ways to think of color as a means to achieve visual hierarchy and/or visual order.

Constructing a Visual Argument—**Basics of Graphic Design as Related to Presentations**

 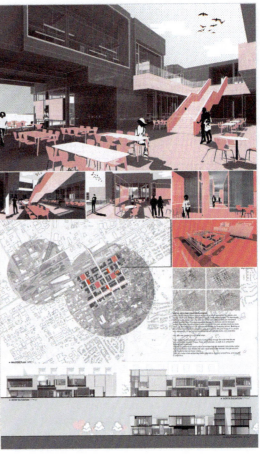

Red and gray are used throughout and provide visual cohesion to elements within the presentation, Neo Urban Studio by Ward Taliaferro.

Using Color for Cohesion
Color implemented within a color family can help an entire board order itself visually. In this case, a color family employed across an entire presentation can visually coalesce the material on the boards. Color families are sets of colors that work together visually without any singular color appearing as most dominant. The use of color families throughout the entire presentation can be seen as an additional way-finding system to make it easier for the reviewer to understand principles of the message. For instance, color could be used to highlight particular segments of text or even parts of the graphics and drawings to draw the reviewer's eye to important elements of the design. All of these applications of color should reinforce established ordering principles of the primary ideas within the presentation.

Color Systems Within a Presentation
It goes without saying that you need to be very purposeful when selecting and using colors to highlight

Keep in mind that black and white is just as powerful a color combination as other color options, from ADAPTABL3 by Jianan Kang.

elements within your presentation. If you use red to highlight text elements for a certain meaning, you can't use red as a program element color because then the reviewer will associate the text that is red to the program element that is also red. Only repeat a color within the presentation if it is representing the same idea. This is a mandatory rule and should not be ignored. Also, be very careful about using colors that are so close in appearance to one another that the reviewer has a hard time visually distinguishing between the two. A full color set should be designed for the entire presentation so that you have enough color types to use for all of the elements you wish to highlight in the design presentation while still maintaining a true family of colors.

If you have multiple boards in a presentation, you still need to relate color families across all of the boards. They should be considered as a designed whole.

Color Matching
Color matching becomes an issue primarily when pulling materials from different software applications. Make sure you are using the same CMYK values—for print—or RGB values—for digital projection—from all design programs so that color families match as they should in the presentation. Also, watch out for instances of mis-matched color when using multiple photographs within the same presentation. Often images taken at different times of day or in different lighting conditions can have very different tonal values. Make sure to work through these issues so they match. One last situation to watch for in particular is with images of models. For instance, if there are three model images of a chipboard model and one image of a white museum board model, there may be color match issues. In this case it might work to convert the images of the chipboard model,

Constructing a Visual Argument—**Basics of Graphic Design as Related to Presentations**

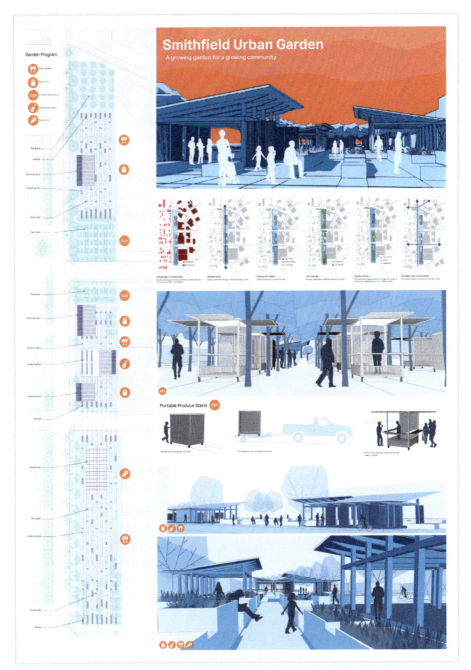

Tones of blue and green with orange as a highlight color work effectively to connect visual material and conceptual ideas in this board presentation, Smithfield Urban Garden: A Growing Garden for a Growing Community by Liz Clark.

Visual Communication for Architects and Designers: constructing the persuasive presentation

Color is used in this presentation drawing to effectively highlight the activity of the interior. New Modes of Dense by Andrea del Pilar Monroig-Torres.

which are very yellow in nature, to black and white to better balance with the other model image, which is predominantly white.

Color versus Black and White
Always remember that black and white are just as colorful as red and blue. Impact occurs when there is a moment of change from an existing system. Consider using monochrome or families of gray to highlight material. Don't just think, "I need to add red!" Often a subtle color change can have a striking impact.

Color to Draw the Eye
Specific application of color can be a powerful tool to draw the eye. Bright or visually noticeable colors—think "highlight"—tend to work best to draw the eye. However, any color that is simply different than other colors used in the presentation can work. Use this tool to your advantage. However, be careful of either drawing the eye in an extreme fashion such that it is difficult to look anywhere else or drawing the eye somewhere you don't want it to go.

Constructing a Visual Argument—Basics of Graphic Design as Related to Presentations

Color families are used to organize design elements and identify them in larger encompassing drawings where multiple design elements are present. Future Foods by Alexis Luna, Guan Yi Chuah and Chit Yee Ng.

Visual Communication for Architects and Designers: constructing the persuasive presentation

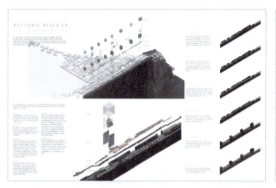

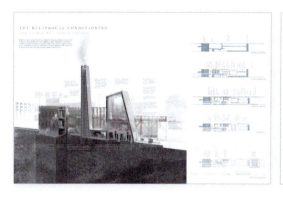

Constructing a Visual Argument—**Basics of Graphic Design as Related to Presentations**

above and left: Dark colors with soft texture work together to create a unifying tactile quality within this presentation, Tilling the Prado: A Furrow of Re-Construction by Ruth McNickle.

Balance versus Symmetry

Balance versus symmetry is a challenging discussion as there are applications of each system that can be quite successful. Because of this, it is difficult to make a clear recommendation. Understanding the difference is perhaps the most straightforward way to proceed.

Symmetry is the easier of the two ideas to explain. A symmetrical layout is one where the organization of content is reflected exactly across a central axis. In layout design the content isn't exactly the same, but the shape of the content is exactly the same.

Pros: A completely symmetrical layout can appear instantly legible because it is so easy to read the order. Symmetry is one of the most understandable forms of order.

Cons: A purely symmetrical layout can stifle the reviewer's capacity to visually enter the content because the balance of white space is exactly the same and the eye has fewer opportunities to roam around the layout. Also, the content of a purely symmetrical layout can be difficult to comprehend because since the order is so easy to recognize, the reviewer may just focus on the shape of the layout rather than on the content included in the layout.

57

Visual Communication for Architects and Designers: constructing the persuasive presentation

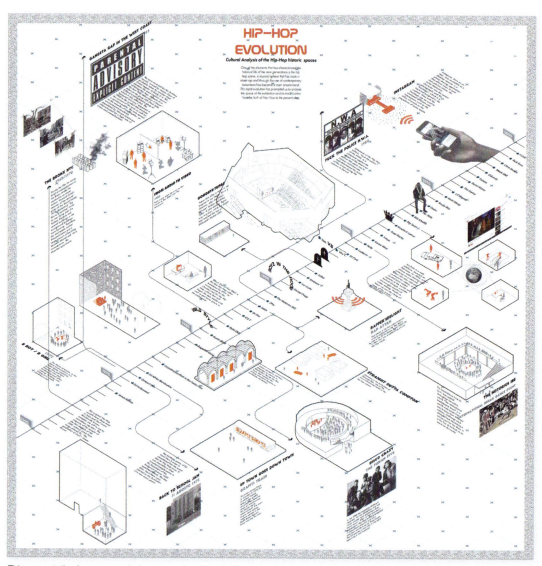

This presentation layout, part of a larger set, demonstrates the ability for text as well as image to operate in three dimensions creating a presentation board that defies the spatial logic of a two-dimensional surface. Drawing selection from Remixing Architecture through Urban Culture, The Bronx Revolution by Andrea Bulloni and Marco Papagni.

A balanced layout relies on the equal distribution of visual weight without the use of symmetry. This design principle depends on the careful arrangement of different elements to successfully push the eye around the presentation while not permitting any one element to stand out as more visually prominent than the others.

Pros: By default, a balanced layout generates varied white space since the layout is altered from symmetry to achieve balance. This varied white space encourages the eye to move freely around the content. More elements are seen and understood through this visual movement.

Cons: It can be quite difficult to achieve a balanced layout when working with strict grids. Incorporating secondary systems of alignments to break an overpowering grid structure can help. Over time and with experience your ability to utilize optical equilibrium to determine if something appears balanced will improve.[11]

Typography

What is typography and why is it so important to your visual argument? Typography is the visual component of written words or, simply stated, how text looks. It is important because, just like visual representations, what words say and how they look when they say it conveys meaning and order. Text in your presentation should support all of the visual elements in the presentation and can add valuable information about the message of the work.

Typically, when you begin designing a presentation, the focus is on the images and drawings needed to convey all of the ideas within your project. These ideas can be further expressed through actual text. Making sure the text in your presentation supports your argument visually is of utmost importance. As with all design projects, there is a vast array of variables that contribute to a successful design presentation. In this section, the art of typography will be discussed exclusively. Don't underestimate the value of working on typographic systems for your presentation; it can make or break the legible cohesion of your design work and argument.

So why can't you just use typefaces that you think look cool? First, there are graphic conventions that pertain to the use of typography in a visual structure—in this case, the design presentation—that are different than typeface conventions previously learned as they relate to writing conventions and visual legibility for something like a writing class. There are also graphic conventions of typography that will greatly enhance the legibility of your visual design argument. It is important to get this correct!

The overall visual structure and thus argument of a presentation depends upon the hierarchical framework created through the considered and pertinent use of typography. Typographic choices can operate as the visual framework for all material on the boards or in the presentation and can help establish overall visual hierarchy. If it is done correctly, the appropriate use of typography can visually direct the reviewer to exactly what you want them to understand about your project.

A design presentation that has been visually weakened through the use of poor typographic practices is easy to identify; it just doesn't look right. The eye is drawn to text rather than to the image content. It is also easy to identify a design presentation that has been visually strengthened through superb use of typographic systems. Here, the eye naturally follows the visual argument and can, with a closer look, read additional information in support of the imagery. Strive for a presentation that visually highlights the important information and uses typeface hierarchy to properly allow the eye to follow the visual direction of the design argument.

So, how do you proceed? Some typographic systems are easier to comprehend and apply than others. There is room for visual choice but, as always, there are just some things that should completely be avoided.

Graphic Rules for Typography

Graphic rules for the written word can have different objectives based on use or application. There are different visual guidelines for typography for something that has more to do with an instructor's ability to read and grade an assignment than rules of graphic legibility. There are different visual guidelines for typography

Visual Communication for Architects and Designers: constructing the persuasive presentation

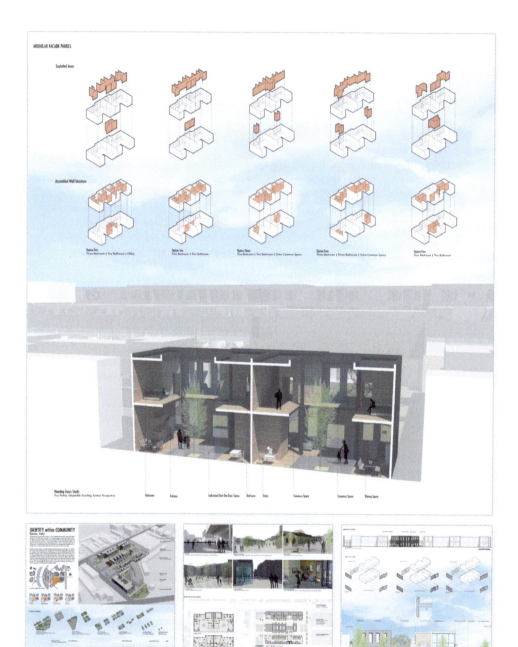

Typeface selection and hierarchy is appropriately used to support the message of the visual representations. Identity Within Community: Rome, Italy by Andie Gamble, Carson Keeney, Tate Lauderdale and Kelsey Wynne.

for something like a newspaper. Different situations can require different applications of the rules. For our purposes to achieve clarity of the visual design message, graphic rules for typography from the profession of graphic design will be followed.[12]

Typeface Selection

The most important thing to remember when selecting a typeface for a presentation is to keep it simple. The images and drawings should be the primary focus of the presentation and the typeface should not overpower them in any way. Also select no more than two or three (at most) different typefaces for use in the entire presentation. The primary typeface can be used for titles. The secondary typeface can be used for all other categories: subtitle, body text, caption and drawing or diagram labels.[13] If a third typeface is absolutely required, relegate it to very specific needs and make sure it is not visually distracting to the rest of the visual hierarchy established through the other typefaces. However, keep in mind appropriate typeface hierarchy is required and can be achieved while using one typeface. See the section on Typeface Range for more information.

Set up a visual hierarchy within the typeface selection that establishes the appropriate visual focus on each typeface while keeping in mind the typeface should always support the visual image and should never overpower your content graphics. Follow this list as a typeface hierarchy guide ranging from most visually prominent to least visually prominent:

1. Title
2. Subtitle
3. Body text
4. Caption
5. Drawing and/or diagram label[14]

Keep in mind that most visually prominent does not necessarily mean the largest typeface or the most bold. All typefaces read differently at different scales and should be evaluated against the system of five hierarchies listed above.

Typeface Range

When selecting a typeface, it is best to try to select one that has a broad visual range. This means that the typeface has at least three ranges of weight—at a minimum you should see a light, medium and bold weight—built into its framework. A spectrum such as this will provide enough visual variance to support an appropriate hierarchy of typefaces within your graphic layout.

If a typeface doesn't have enough hierarchical range to fulfill all of your graphic organizational needs, before you rush to add another typeface, first try to reduce the amount of black in the typeface thus creating a lighter body of text in gray. Basically, you can use gray colored text within the same typeface: this is a very effective tool and automatically establishes a hierarchical relationship between the black text and the gray text.

Serif versus Sans Serif and Arguments of Visual Legibility

When it comes to determining legibility based on the selection of serif or sans serif typefaces, there are several different schools of thought. First, let's define the difference. Individual characters in a serif typeface have serifs associated with them; a serif is a small line attached to the end of a stroke in a letter. Typefaces that have this additional line are called serif typefaces and typefaces without this additional line are called sans serif typefaces.

Making the determination about which style to select depends completely on the legibility of the typeface at the actual size it will be used in the presentation. Some designers contend that serif typefaces are visually more accessible because the serif makes it easier to recognize the shape of words and therefore is more legible than sans serif typefaces. Others argue that sans serif typefaces are visually cleaner than serif typefaces and consequently are easier to read.

Determine typeface selection by testing different typefaces in your presentation to decide which is best. Be aware that it is not enough to test typeface legibility on the computer screen. For physical presentations, you will need to print the presentation at the correct scale, pin it up on the wall and view it from the correct distance—at least 5 feet away or 1.5 meters. For a digital presentation—even a digitally projected board layout—you must test it on the screen size and scenario in which it will be viewed. Select the typeface that is the most visually legible without being distracting to the image content in the presentation.

Uppercase versus Lowercase

It is not a good idea to use all uppercase letters in a long body of text. The reason is this; the human eye uses typographic ascenders and descenders found in lowercase letters as a visual reference to help identify words by the actual shape of the word while simultaneously reading the word letter by letter. Ascenders extend above the mean line and descenders extend below the baseline. When a paragraph of text is in all uppercase letters, it is not as easy for the reader to recognize the shape of the word and it becomes more challenging to read the body of text. Uppercase is fine for titles and can effectively be utilized in just about any situation except for full sentences or paragraphs where reading at speed with comprehension is needed.

X-Height Variations

X-height is essentially the letter height that determines the mean line for each specific typeface. As its name suggests, it is the height of the lowercase x which in turn is the general height of all lowercase letters excluding those with ascenders and descenders. The x-height is significant because the x-height of a letter is how designers measure the visual weight of the typeface. Remember, when selecting a typeface be cautious and aware that typefaces that are the same size will most likely have a different visual weight because of the differences between the x-heights.

Underlining, Bold and Italics

Understanding and following the guidelines for underlying, bold and italics are simple. Use bold and italics to expand the visual range of typeface selections. However, you should completely avoid underlining words and passages in your text. Underlining creates a harsh line within the visual space of a paragraph and detracts from the legibility of the text.

Text Rivers

Text rivers are white spaces that show up over multiple lines of text occurring either between sentences or within irregular spacing between words. Text rivers can create a visible pattern in the text paragraph making it more difficult to read. You can avoid text rivers by making sure that you consistently have a single space after each sentence rather than a double space. Text rivers can also create a visual problem when setting a body of text to a justified width. Justified text creates a strong vertical alignment at both the right and left edges of a paragraph. In order to maintain this alignment, the spaces between words are adjusted to many different lengths. This adjustment will more often than not create significant rivers within the text.

Kerning and Tracking

Kerning is manually adjusting the space between letters in a word. It is used primarily by graphic designers to correct irregular spaces created through the adjacencies between some specific letters such as when a capital A and a capital W are next to one another in a word.

Tracking is manually adjusting the general space between letters and words in a larger piece of text and not just between individual letters in a word, as is the case with kerning.

Here's what you need to know. Working with kerning and tracking depends on a combination of subtle moves and should not be noticeable to the eye when looking at a body of text. If you find yourself using kerning or tracking to force a piece of text to fit in a certain space by either spacing it out to make it longer or compressing it to make it smaller means the tools are being used incorrectly. If more text is needed to fill a space, write more text. If less text is needed in a visual space, edit it.

Leading

The term leading refers to a time when actual pieces of lead were used to create spaces between lines of metal type. As you can imagine, leading is the art

Constructing a Visual Argument—**Basics of Graphic Design as Related to Presentations**

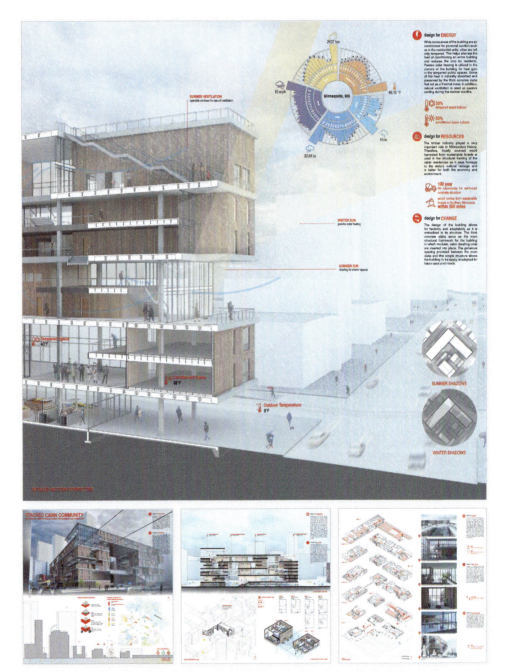

Color within the typeface hierarchy system is used to highlight important ideas relevant to the design objectives. Stacked Cabin Community: Sustainable Urban Living in Downtown Minneapolis, Minnesota by Roberto Diaz Manzanares and Hawraa Charara.

Visual Communication for Architects and Designers: constructing the persuasive presentation

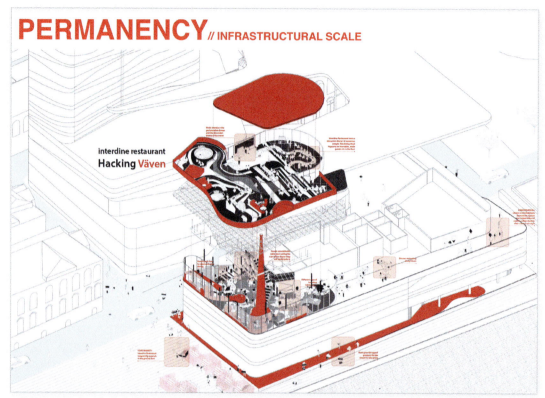

above and right: Color and consistency in the typeface hierarchy system are effectively used to support the visual legibility of this presentation. Drawing selections from Interdine by Gaia Crocella.

of adjusting the vertical spacing between full lines of text. Adjusting the leading can be extremely helpful in managing visual weight within a piece of text. Be careful of overuse; issues similar to those that exist for kerning and tracking can arise. Making the leading too large can make a paragraph difficult to read because there is little visual connectivity line to line; making the leading too tight can make a paragraph difficult to read because the lines are not visually separate enough and everything tends to run together. Leading is generally measured baseline to baseline.

There are more visual reasons to adjust the leading than either kerning or tracking. Lean on leading to make visual space adjustments for pieces of text.

Measure

Measure is defined as the number of characters (including spaces) in a line of text. Measure matters because it challenges legibility. Extreme examples of measure—paragraphs of text that seem awkwardly narrow in width and paragraphs of text that seem awkwardly wide—make it very difficult to read through multiple lines of text. If the width of the paragraph is too narrow, reading line to line becomes jumpy because the eye is forced to return to the start of the next line multiple times within a short amount of conceptual space. If the paragraph is too wide, the eye physically gets lost as it returns to the start of the next line. Luckily, there is a clear guideline for this. For single column bodies of text, use between 45 and 75 characters per line; something

Constructing a Visual Argument—**Basics of Graphic Design as Related to Presentations**

around 65 is usually about right. For multi-column bodies of text, 40 to 50 characters per line is optimal. Of course, these rules have some variations depending on the typeface that is being used. Keep the guidelines in mind and strive to get as close to the measure recommendations as possible.

Text Alignment

Selecting a text alignment style can be tricky. Often, design students simply default to text blocks justified left and right. While it is understandable why that would be selected—it gives a straight vertical edge at both the right and left edges of the text block for aligning other items—it is not always the best choice. See below to review the text alignment options and to learn the pros and cons of each choice.

Rag Right (also called Justified Left): A paragraph of text set to rag right means that it is aligned to the left and is not aligned on the right leaving the right text edge uneven—thus the label rag.

Pros: Rag right is the most typically used text alignment style and is easily legible because the left side aligns at the same edge with each line of text. With rag right, the eye always knows where each line of text begins at the left, justified edge.

Cons: Rag right can be visually problematic when the rag edge is either overrun with hyphenated word breaks or is very dramatically uneven. Both of these issues need to be visually managed when working with a rag right text alignment style.

Visual Communication for Architects and Designers: constructing the persuasive presentation

Rag Left (also called Justified Right): A paragraph of text set to rag left means that it is aligned to the right and is not aligned on the left leaving the left text edge uneven—thus the label rag.

Pros: Rag left provides a straight hard right edge that can emphasize a prominent right-hand edge in a layout.

Cons: Rag left can be difficult to read particularly for a large block of text. When reading, the eye registers back to the left edge of text to start reading the next line of text. When using rag left, this "start" location jumps around right and left and makes it more challenging to read and comprehend the text.

Justified: A paragraph of text that is justified is aligned on both the right and the left edges of the text.

Pros: Justified text allows for both a strong right and left edge which makes it very easy to visually align material to the text block.

Cons: Be mindful when using justified text. This alignment style sets the tracking of the paragraph line by line so that it aligns as a straight edge on both the right and left sides of the block of text. In an effort to make the spacing between words and letters as even as possible with justified text, often a preponderance of word breaks (hyphens) occur at the end of each line. This can be incredibly visually distracting as the vertical alignment of repeated hyphens begins to show up at the right edge. To remedy this, try setting the paragraph style in Adobe InDesign to "no hyphen." This will solve the word break issue as no words will break at the end of each line. However, now a new issue will emerge; the characters and words on each line will be spaced differently to accommodate a static line width in conjunction with a completely different set of characters on each line. This forced alignment and automatic tracking creates large gaps, called text rivers, in the body of the text and can be visually distracting. Test both with and without the "no hyphen" setting and decide what is most visually legible. It could possibly be a combination of both settings.

Centered: A paragraph of text that is centered means just what it says; each line of text is centered about a central axis.

Pros: Centered text can create a sense of centered balance on a page.

Cons: Centered text should not be used for paragraphs of text. It is visually illegible for large arrangements of text and does not give any edges to align images or drawings to in your presentation layout. The left edge is particularly problematic for legibility purposes because it shifts back and forth to accommodate the center, making the paragraph of text incredibly difficult to read as the starting point of each line is constantly changing. Successfully using centered text in design presentations is very challenging and it should be avoided.

Orphans, Widows and Runts

An orphan is a single line of text left by itself at the bottom of a column of text. A widow is a single line of text left alone at the top of a column of text. A runt is a single word on a line by itself at the end of a paragraph.

Neither orphans, widows nor runts are acceptable and all diminish the legibility of a body of text. Fix them! It is tempting to ignore these guidelines but nothing makes a layout appear more sophomoric than overlooking these rules.

Constructing a Visual Argument—**Basics of Graphic Design as Related to Presentations**

Established typeface hierarchy provides clear indication of prominent design ideas and draws the eye to the appropriate design elements. Future Residential Paradigm for Rome by Alexander Michael Hamady, Prakhar Singh, Dongkyu Yoon and Boyu Xiao.

Visual Communication for Architects and Designers: constructing the persuasive presentation

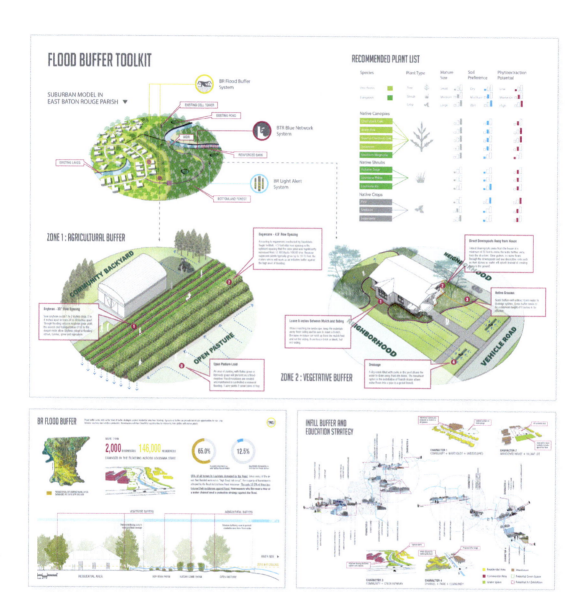

Highlight color, in this case pink, is used to draw the eye to important information—call-out boxes and key numbers—and ties all three of these boards together graphically. As part of a larger set, these drawing selections are from Disaster Autopsy Model by Donguk Lee and Xiwei Shen.

Graphic Punctuation

There are a handful of punctuation rules and styles that every designer should be aware of and should implement. These are often different from things you've been taught in the past but are commonly known to all graphic designers. These particular rules regarding punctuation and style have graphic consequences and should be applied to improve the visual order of the presentation. Don't ignore them, they are all an easy fix and avoiding them makes your presentation look unprofessional.

Dashes
There are actually three different types of dashes and all have very specific applications. Learn the differences between a hyphen, an en dash and an em dash.

Hyphen
A hyphen is the smallest of the dashes and is primarily used in compound word construction: self-evident. The other instance where a hyphen is often used is in a telephone number.

En Dash
An en dash is of medium length and is only used when describing a range in time or numbers: 1999–2001 or pages 34–45.

Em Dash
An em dash is the longest of the dashes and is used in sentence structure to set apart a phrase: Broccoli, bananas and beets—these are some of the things I need from the store.

Of the three dashes, the em dash is most flexible. A hyphen is only for compound word construction or telephone numbers; an en dash is only for number ranges. Basically, an em dash is a piece of punctuation that is used for any other application. Do not use hyphens or en dashes for anything other than what they are intended.

There are no spaces either before or after the hyphen, en dash or em dash.

Ellipsis
An ellipsis is a piece of punctuation used to indicate a portion of text has been removed. It is also acceptable to use an ellipsis to indicate a pause or moment of thought in a written statement. Do not use the automatically generated ellipsis from your word processing program. A proper ellipsis is formed like this: word dot space dot space dot space. . .

Lists and Bullets
Typesetting lists is a challenge. Often bullets are needed to move the eye properly down a list. Sometimes bullets that are automatically generated through your writing program can create an overpowering visual line of large dots on the page. To correct this issue, delete the automatically generated dots and redraw them in Adobe InDesign as much smaller dots. Another option is to simply create a list graphically by separating each item with changes in leading (the space between the lines of text). Test both methods and make a choice based on whether or not the dots are too visually distracting.

Hyphen Settings for Paragraphs
In the paragraph settings menu in Adobe InDesign you can decide when to turn hyphen settings on or off for a body of text. Basically, this setting regulates whether or not words break at the end of a line of text by inserting a hyphen. When using rag right or rag left, turn off the hyphen settings so the risk of having multiple end-of-line hyphens appearing is removed. Test the hyphen settings with justified text to determine a balance between end of line word breaks, and thus hyphens, and the aggressive spacing adjustments causing text rivers that appear without it.

Paragraph Indentation
When writing large bodies of text, paragraph breaks need to be inserted to set apart different parts of a verbal argument. At the beginning of a new paragraph do not indent the first line of text. Paragraph indentation creates an additional and blocky rag edge to the left side of the body of text. This irregular white space is visually distracting to the other orders being established on the page. Instead, when you begin a new paragraph, use a single line of separation between each paragraph.[15]

presentation conventions for architecture

constructing a visual argument

In the rush to finish a presentation it is easy to forget basic principles related to architectural symbols and drawing conventions. However, it is imperative that you remember these rules and include them with all architectural drawings. It will make the difference between a presentation that represents a designer's understanding of how architectural systems work together and one that just has the designer checking the box of drawings they must complete. This is an important difference!

During the course of project development, often several different graphic styles might be used to study different aspects of the design. After all, we know that some tools are simply better for certain tasks. The same holds true for design representations. Some things just work better to study specific scenarios. For instance, there may be a mix of hand-drawn representations and digital representations. When applying architectural symbols and conventions to a mix of drawing and representation types, don't stress too much about the fact that there are differences within your representation styles. Do your best to make your symbols and conventions look cohesive. For a presentation design it is completely acceptable to mix drawing and representation types; in fact, it may make more sense. Different style representations can express different ideas. So, the rule of thumb is to match symbols and conventions where appropriate. Make sure they are included everywhere because inclusion is not only appropriate, it's mandatory.

Visual Communication for Architects and Designers: constructing the persuasive presentation

Symbols and Conventions

North Arrow

Within your presentation, you must include a north arrow for every site plan and ground floor plan. This is not optional, but required. There are a wide variety of acceptable north arrows; select one that makes the most visual sense with the graphic sensibilities of the entire presentation. Use the same north arrow style everywhere one is needed in the presentation.

Graphic Scale

When projects are developed, they are usually represented at a normative architectural scale: 1/4" = 1', 1cm = 0.5m, etc. This architectural scale only makes sense when the drawings are printed to scale. An architectural scale makes no sense if it is presented digitally as it is only a reference for printed works. Therefore, the rules governing the label definition of scale vary between print strategies and digital strategies.

Graphic Scale in Printed Presentations
For a printed presentation, the ideal scenario is to maintain a true architectural scale when presenting your drawings. This means scaling your drawings to a true architectural scale: 1/4" = 1', 1cm = 0.5m, etc. However, sometimes it becomes necessary to present a drawing at a reduced scale so that all of the required materials fit within the presentation.

When architectural scales are no longer correct to a normative scale, it actually doesn't make sense to try to figure out what they are at the reduced scale. Something like 5/64" = 1' isn't an architectural scale and therefore isn't measurable with an architectural tool. At this point it is necessary to use a graphic scale—also called a bar scale—for all the drawings in the presentation. The best way to ensure the bar scale is correct relative to the scale of the drawing is to draw the bar scale correctly with the original drawing and then keep the bar scale and drawing together as a unit and scale the entire unit so that both drawing and bar scale are scaled together. Since the bar scale travels with the drawing as it is reproduced at any scale, it always maintains a correct scalar relationship to the drawing and can be used as a mini-measuring device to determine dimensions on the drawing as needed.

Graphic Scale in Digital Presentations
For digital presentations, writing out an architectural scale, for instance as part of a caption, makes no sense. This is because you can't use an architectural measuring tool (your scale) to physically measure something that is being displayed at any number of sizes depending on how it is viewed digitally. For digital presentations, a bar scale must always be used. There are no exceptions to this rule. See discussion above for best practices on maintaining the correct bar scale with your digital drawing.

Again, there are a variety of ways to draw a bar scale. Choose the one that is most in line with the graphic sensibilities employed and use this same bar scale style for all locations in the presentation.

Section Cut Lines

Section cut lines on plans are a requirement for your presentation. For your plans and sections to make sense together, plans need section cut lines to mark where the building sections are cut. Ideally section cut lines should be repeated on every single plan level.

Section cut lines can be drawn a variety of ways. However, it is important to make sure that the section cut lines are neither distracting to the legibility of the plan nor invisible. Both scenarios are problematic. There are subtle yet legible ways to draw section cut lines; do not let them pull your eye in any way. If the cut lines go all the way through the plan, they need to be a very light, solid or dashed line in a dash that is different than any other dashed line type on the drawing set. If you draw section cut lines as a solid line make sure it is a very thin line or you run the risk of the cut lines conflating with the actual lines in the drawing. If possible, it is better if the cut lines do not go all the way through the plan drawing and instead stay outside the primary space of the plan.

Don't forget to also pay attention to the style of the view direction indicator at each end of the section cut line. Stick with something like a streamlined rectangular bar perpendicular to the section cut line. Avoid arrows as direction indicators. An arrow used as a direction indicator will always draw the eye to the arrow—it seems visually out of place against other orthogonal lines in the drawing.

Drawing and Diagram Call-Out Leader Lines

Drawing and diagram call-out leader lines are the lines drawn to attach a small bit of text—a call-out—to the part of the drawing it is directly describing. These call-outs can be an ideal way to direct the reviewer's attention to a very specific portion of a drawing, diagram or image. They allow the designer to describe something that might otherwise get missed as the reviewer is visually scanning the content. The challenge lies in the graphic representation of the actual leader lines. These lines should be very thin, solid lines. They should be drawn in a way that does not get confused with actual lines in the drawing or diagram. The rule of thumb is that if the leader lines cross over a drawing or diagram with orthographic lines—lines in perpendicular relationships—don't use straight horizontal or vertical lines for the leader lines unless the line type is distinctly different. Another option is to draw the leader lines at an angle so they do not get confused with actual lines in the drawing or diagram. If the leader lines do not cross over orthographic lines or are used for an image; it is permissible to draw the leader lines as straight horizontal or vertical lines. In either case, the lines should be straight, not curved. Dashed or dotted lines might work as well but make sure the dash or dot is subtle enough so as not to be visually distracting.

Visually Stack the Plan Drawings

There is definitely a correct way to arrange plans in a presentation and this rule must be followed unless there is simply no way to make it work due to presentation or drawing constraints. The most correct way to stack plans is to have the bottom level at the bottom of the stack and move up through the floors in sequential order above this bottom level. When looking at plans organized in this manner, the reviewer is able to visually collapse the drawings onto one another to get a three-dimensional understanding of the building. If plans are not organized in this way, you are asking the reviewer to do a lot of unnecessary work to try to visually piece together your building. This will take time away from the actual ideas of your project.

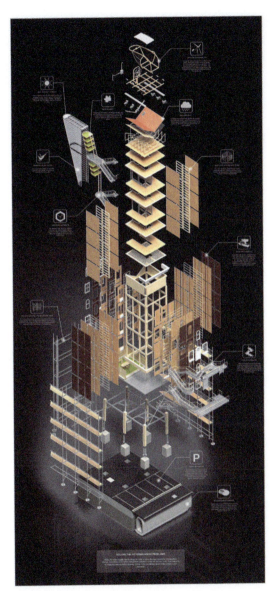

Call-outs point to specific areas of relevance in the drawing amplifying a reviewer's understanding of fundamental design elements. Drawing selection is titled Solving the Victorian House Problems from the project, The D.I.Y. Building by Paul-Andrei Burghelea.

There will be occasions when it is simply not possible to correctly stack the plan drawings due to size limitations or requirements in the presentation. When this happens, try not to worry about it too much. Make logical choices keeping the idea about visually collapsing the drawings in mind.[16]

Labeling Systems

Labeling systems in both print and digital presentations need to operate in a hierarchical set. See the section on Typography for reference. Getting the typeface hierarchy incorrect can lead to immense visual confusion within the presentation. Getting the hierarchy incorrect can also cause all reviewer eyes to be distracted with the visual presence of words and prevent them from actually seeing the representations and ultimately can prevent them from understanding your design project.

Drawing and Diagram Titles

All drawings and diagrams included in the presentation need titles. These titles reinforce the objective of the drawing, and are another way to direct the reviewer to exactly what they should understand about the project. Including drawing and diagram titles in your presentation is vital. Without them, it is impossible for the reviewer to understand your intent behind a drawing or diagram.

For example, there is a distinct difference between these two diagram labels—first, "spatial diagram" and second, "spatial diagram of the relationship between interior void and exterior void." See the difference? The first diagram title just lists the obvious. The second diagram title tells the reviewer how they should be studying the diagram. The first simply notes that you know what kind of diagram it is. The second shows that there is intention behind your work. This is an important distinction. See the section on Text in Your Presentation to better understand verbal and visual goals for each type of text within your presentation.

Plan Program Labels

There are several acceptable ways to label programmatic elements in a set of plan drawings. For some reason people feel very strongly about how this should be done and often make strict rules about it. The truth is that each method has pros and cons and the real answer about which you should use is. . . it depends. Determine what makes the most sense for what you are trying to accomplish. Either one—if done correctly—can be effective and beautiful. Remember to test your drawing legibility at the scale and at the distance it will be viewed; this applies to both printed and digital presentations.

Option One: Include the program labels directly on plan

Pros: Including the program labels directly on the plan makes it simple to quickly understand programmatic relationships because the reviewer is simultaneously reading the spatial plan and the written program.

Cons: Including the program labels directly on the plan can be quite distracting to the legibility of the actual plan. It's a graphic problem of visual hierarchy.

Solution: To make this approach work, you'll need to do a series of studies to work out the correct visual hierarchy between the legibility of the plan and the legibility of the program labels. It is most important to make the plan legible; this is your first priority. The program labels must be visually subservient to the legibility of the plan while still being legible themselves. Start here: increase the visual strength of the line work or poché where the plan has been cut by making them darker or more visually prominent. Then reduce the visual weight of the program labels by using a sans serif typeface, reducing the size of the typeface and experimenting with a gray tone instead of full black. All labels included in the drawing should be aligned with other labels used in the plan. Do this step to ensure that they are placed in an orderly fashion.

Option Two: List program labels in a key located adjacent to the plan

Pros: Listing the program labels in a key located adjacent to the plan visually opens the plan drawing because the only additional elements on the plan are small letters or numbers. There is less visual clutter to distract from the legibility of the plan.

Cons: Listing the program labels in a key located adjacent to the plan forces reviewers to constantly move their eyes between the plan and the key. This can reduce their immediate understanding of the plan.

Constructing a Visual Argument—**Presentation Conventions for Architecture**

White poché, subtle color and appropriate typeface use make these plans spatially legible. Drawing selection from Sol' nad zlato: Introducing an Inclusive Strategy for Resilient Development of the Neglected Regions in Slovakia by Katarina Zatkova.

Solution: For this to work, the program key must be located directly adjacent to the drawing it is referencing with no other visual information between the list and the drawing. Add numbers or letters to the program list so you can include just those numbers or letters on the plan. Make sure the numbers or letters located in the plan are arranged in an orderly fashion—literally in order and aligned with other numbers or letters in the plan as appropriate.

Option Three: Use call-outs and leader lines to attach program to the plan

Pros: With this option, leader lines point directly to the program locations on the plan and precisely tie program words to the drawing.

Cons: The primary con for this option is that the leader lines can become visually distracting as they cross over the lines in the plan drawing.

Solution: The best way to make this scenario work is to very carefully design the style of the leader lines. They should not be the same as any line type in the drawing. Sometimes a dashed or dotted line will work but be careful about this as too many dashed lines can also be visually distracting. Often a very thin, straight line works best. Make sure to angle the leader lines if needed so they don't get confused with lines in the drawing. Vertically align your program labels at either the right or left edge, depending on what side of the drawing they are on, and use this aligned edge as the point of contact with the leader line.

Secondary Diagram Labels and Call-Outs

Always remember to include secondary diagram labels and call-outs. These secondary labels support the message of the primary labels and are invaluable toward the delivery of the design message. Remember, the reviewer doesn't always know what seems obvious to the designer.[17]

Visual Communication for Architects and Designers: constructing the persuasive presentation

IDENTIFYING CULTURAL COMPONENTS OF THE CITY

Vertical leader lines coupled with representational figures annotate this cultural view of the city with spatial and typological clarity. Drawing selection from Dichotomy of Kyoto by Ayah Hatahet. To review additional work from this project, see page 89.

Constructing a Visual Argument—**Presentation Conventions for Architecture**

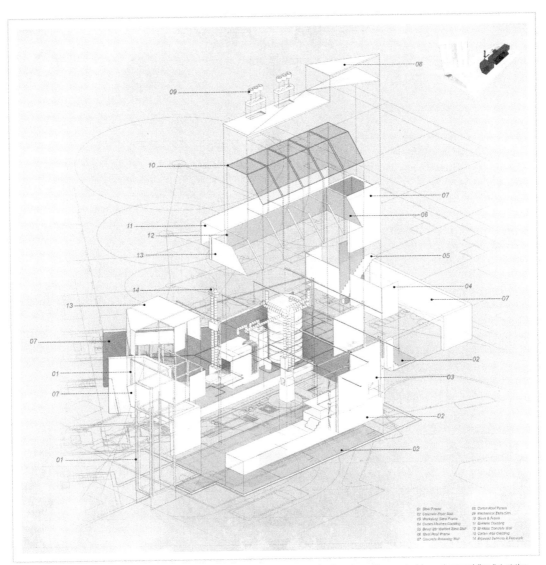

The complexity of this explanatory drawing is organized through the use of leader lines keyed to a materials and assemblies list at the lower right. Drawing selection from Integrated Metal Workshop by James Mason.

Visual Communication for Architects and Designers: constructing the persuasive presentation

78

Constructing a Visual Argument—**Presentation Conventions for Architecture**

above: For this drawing titled New Facilities and Arrival Platform, color coding of activity types animates the exploded axonometric describing the spatial relationship between levels of the proposal.

left: For the drawing titled Past, Present and Future Events, a subtle application of call-outs and leader lines allows the drawing to maintain visual priority while including relevant annotations.

Drawing selections from The Chatterley Platform by Samuel Letchford.

Visual Legibility of Presentation Drawings

There are a lot of issues to keep in mind when you are preparing drawings for presentation. The first thing to realize is that software designed for the construction industry—AutoCAD, Revit and similar—is designed for the purpose of construction legibility and isn't always the best tool for preparing presentation drawings. For presentation drawings you want to work with software that is designed for easy and fluid line work and tone flexibility—Adobe Illustrator and similar. Design legibility in presentation line drawings demands a specific set of legibility conventions and requires adjustments to be made to the drawings to ensure clear understanding of spatial conditions described in the two-dimensional drawings.

Another challenge when placing architectural drawings within a presentation is dealing with spatial legibility as related to drawing scale. Each time a drawing is produced, there are legibility conventions associated with the specific scale it is drawn. For instance, if a drawing is produced to be reviewed at 1/4" = 1' or 1cm = 0.5m, there is a set of legibility conventions followed for presenting at that scale. If the drawing has been reduced significantly to fit within size requirements for a printed presentation or for a digital presentation, drawing changes will be required to maintain spatial clarity at the new scale in the presentation. Below is a list of operations that need to be addressed. These operations are primarily for orthographic drawings—plan, section, elevation—but look through all other drawings in the presentation for issues as well.

Remember, these operations have to be reviewed at the actual size that each drawing will appear in the final presentation and applies to both printed and digital presentations. It won't work to make these adjustments first and then resize the drawing for the presentation to see how it looks. That defeats the point. Work and review in the actual size the drawings will be in the presentation.

Line Weight

Line weight is one of the most important things to get correct for the legibility of drawings in a presentation. The rules are commonly known, but below is a quick guide to follow. And remember, review the drawings at the scale they are displayed in the presentation to be able to make these line weight adjustments. Use no more than five line weights:

1. Line weight 01 is the darkest and should be used to indicate the planes that have been cut through.

2. Line weight 02 is slightly lighter than 01 and indicates those edges closest to the planes that were cut.

3. Line weight 03 is slightly lighter than 02 and indicates those edges beyond those drawn with line weight 02.

4. Line weight 04 is slightly lighter than 03 and indicates those edges beyond those drawn with line weight 03.

5. Line weight 05 is reserved for construction lines and should be the absolute lightest line.[18]

Applying this simple system can alleviate struggles when trying to figure out what line weight to use. Any line weight hierarchy beyond the five described above will actually begin to confuse the drawing and it will start to lose visual qualities of spatial depth.

Contour Lines and Context in Plan

When drawing the ground floor plan of a project, typically the site or context is drawn as well. This material shows how the project connects to its context. When contour lines are included in this context, make certain that the contour lines are an appropriately scaled line. For that matter, both contour lines and contextual lines should be visually lighter than other lines on the ground floor plan so that they will visually act as support information.

Poché

Usually an architectural presentation is made to a group of people. This group could vary radically in size from a small review of four or five people to a large audience of 100 or more. The thing both of these presentation sizes have in common, whether a printed presentation or a digital presentation, is that the reviewers are located at a distance from the drawings. And since the drawings in your presentation are viewed from some distance, it is a good idea to add poché, if it isn't already there,

Constructing a Visual Argument—**Presentation Conventions for Architecture**

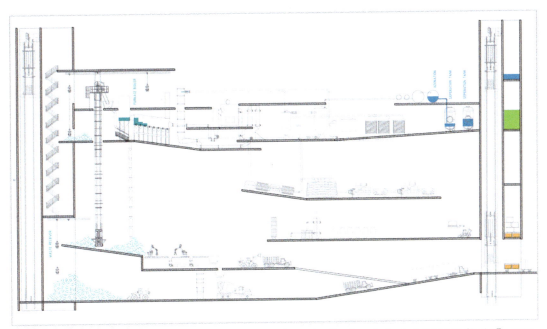

Precise line work and line weight with soft poché give depth to this active section. Drawing selection from Measures: Circular Economy Infrastructure + Institution, A Generative Design Methodology by Edward Palka and Abraham Murrell.

to the planes that are cut through in plan and section. Sometimes simple line weights without poché will work and still convey spatial zones in the drawing. But step back and try to look at them through the eyes of someone who is not familiar with the drawings. The point of poché is to make it easier for the eye to travel from space to space within the drawings. If you can't see the edge of the space—if just line weight and no poché is used—either radically improve the legibility of the line weights or go ahead and add poché. Typically, poché works best. The poché can be black or a gray tone or even a color. Poché coupled with the proper line weights will greatly increase the legibility of all drawings.

Hatch

Using hatch to denote a tone for a spatial zone can be problematic. Hatching is a series of lines in a pattern to create the illusion of a solid tone and is a style setting that comes from AutoCAD and should be avoided in a presentation drawing. Hatch has difficulty scaling and creates uncontrollable moiré patterns when reduced, printed or projected. If a drawing needs a solid tone—for poché, or to describe floor plates or program zones—draw a solid tone in Adobe Illustrator. There are more options in Adobe Illustrator and you'll have greater flexibility to adjust color and opacity.

Compound Line Edits

Often multiple, close-together lines are needed in a plan, section or elevation to represent different types of spatial situations. There are several examples of this scenario: multiple lines at a window cut in plan or section where two lines are shown for the glass cut with lines for the sill or wall edge beyond, or the multiple lines at a run of stairs in plan. These sets of lines make sense when they are viewed zoomed in on the screen or printed at the scale they were drawn. However, when they are printed or projected at a smaller size for presentation, be careful, because these sets of lines can compound and instead of reading like a series of very thin lines, they can read as one thick line. These compound lines essentially inverse the line weight relationship between

Visual Communication for Architects and Designers: constructing the persuasive presentation

White poché supports the legibility of spaces within this section by highlighting and framing them in opposition to the rendered tone of the drawing. Drawing selection from #RIP: Encoding Memory by Mai Abusalih, Eric Giragosian and Min He.

things like the wall and the window. Because of this inversion, when showing a plan, section or elevation for a presentation, remove some of the multiple lines at these types of locations so that they read visually thinner. There are several detailed areas in your drawings where this can be a problem. It is especially an issue when you import standard fixtures, etc. into a drawing. Things like toilet handles or sink faucets are notorious for creating compound line issues when a drawing is reduced in scale making a toilet handle or sink faucet the most prominent item in the drawing.[19]

Arrows

Arrows in drawings are visually challenging. Since arrows are typically a completely different shape than anything else found in the drawing, they can be very visually distracting. You need to reduce their visual weight by adjusting them in a variety of ways. Arrows are so visually distracting in orthographic drawings that I avoid them entirely. But if you must include them, follow these guidelines to adjust the visual weight of the arrows in your presentation drawings:

1. Make sure the arrow head is appropriate for the drawing. Stay away from cartoon-like, soft-edged arrows in orthographic drawings. Also avoid arrow heads that are pure, geometric triangles; these are equally distracting because they have a geometric structure that competes with the geometric structures found in the drawings. Instead, look for arrows that have pointed edges not soft edges and have elongated triangle-shaped heads.

2. Make sure the stroke of the arrow is not too thick. There should be a perfect balance between the stroke of the arrow and the head of the arrow. If either one is not in the correct proportional relationship, the arrow will be

Constructing a Visual Argument—**Presentation Conventions for Architecture**

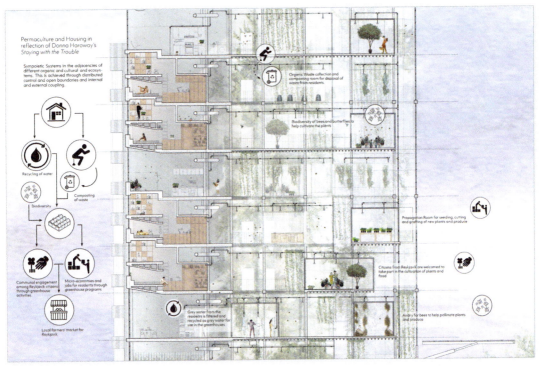

Discreet, clean arrows of appropriate scale and style work within the support diagram to this systems section. Drawing selection from Ecosystems of [That] Matter by Abena Bonna.

too visually prominent simply because it looks strange to the eye and will be visually distracting.

3. Make sure the arrow is in proper proportion with the overall drawing. Too large or too small in relation to the scale of the drawing will also be visually distracting.

4. And finally, the arrow should be reduced in tone so it does not read as strongly as the actual line and poché of the drawing.[20]

Door Swings

Door swings are one of the greatest challenges in plan drawing legibility. Door swings are an important element to include in your plan drawings because they convey how one enters or exits a space and they display understanding of egress constraints. However, the challenge is this; door swing lines are not real lines. They don't exist in physical space. They are merely an indication of the movement of the door.

Using a solid line for a door swing in plan can be the single most distracting element in the plan. Solid line door swings completely block the visible flow of space by stopping the eye's ability to roam in and out of spaces within the plan. Door swings in general are prominent curved elements in the drawing that stand out against a typically orthogonal drawing.

Luckily, there are several effective ways to correct these issues. The challenge is to retain the eye's ability to move through the drawing and spatially connect all of the zones of the plan. Every time the eye hits a solid door swing, it stops and has to jump to the next space, effectively destroying any spatial continuity you are trying to convey.

Make the door swings visually diminished enough that the eye can pass through them. Here are the options:

Visual Communication for Architects and Designers: constructing the persuasive presentation

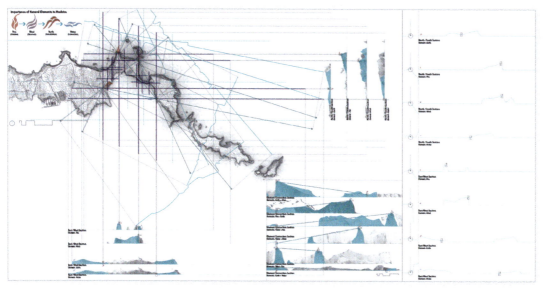

This complex drawing of multiple sections of the site plan is ordered through projection lines with drawn section categories grouped together. Importance of Natural Elements in Madeira by Caroline Niederpruem.

1. Remove the door swings completely. However, leave the actual doors open.

2. Change the door swing line to a very thin line.

3. Change the door swing line to a very thin dashed or dotted line.

4. Change the door swing line to a reduced opacity so it is not solid black.

5. Change the door swing line to a combination of any of the above.[21]

Floor Plate Clarity in Plan: Marking Spaces that Are Open to Below

Marking spaces in plan that are open to below is a great way to connect double or triple height spaces between floor plates. Remember the discussion about properly stacking plans in a presentation so the reviewer can collapse the plans and understand how things work together? Marking spaces that are voids in the building also helps the reviewers understand spatial connectivity between floors. There are a handful of ways to make these vertical spatial connections legible. One is to simply write "open to below" directly over the open space in the plan drawing. When adding any words to the plan, make sure to follow rules of legibility and don't allow the weight or size of these words distract from the visual legibility of the plan. The other thing to try is to place color tone in the plan that denotes the actual floor plate. This will effectively leave the vertical voids blank, thus helping the reviewer spatially connect them.

Be careful when using a pair of diagonal lines crossing the open space to denote there is an open to below condition. Standard conventions say that crossed diagonal lines in plan should only be used at mechanical chase locations—spaces that are not physically accessible in plan. These chases are typically vertical mechanical spaces and are not occupiable. Do not use these diagonal crossed lines for voids in your plan that denote a designed spatial condition. If there is a large "X" on the plan over these spaces, it becomes impossible to understand that the space visually continues across the plan.

Image Quality Issues

Make sure that all images included in the presentation are high quality; they must be at an acceptable level of image resolution. Basically, this means if it is noticeable that something is off in the image, it is not acceptable to use. Images that are over-scaled in relation to their resolution will appear pixelated. Do not include any images with distinct, visible pixelation in the presentation.

Image Focus

All photographic images used in your presentation must be properly focused. All images that are blurred through an error in photography must be removed. However, it is permissible to use an image that has a very deep focal point; this will make portions of the foreground blurred. Use this technique when trying to identify something deep in the spatial range of an image. But be careful that the foregrounded blur isn't visually distracting.

Line Work in Raster Files

Verify that all line work in drawings that are raster files is legible when printed or projected at the correct size for the presentation. Hand-drawn drawings that have been digitally scanned are notoriously difficult to successfully adjust in Adobe Photoshop. Be very careful that lines are not lost as you are trying to remove tone from the background of the drawing.

Rich Black Issue

Rich black is a color formula used in printing to achieve a more intense, deep black. There are several acceptable formulas for rich black; a common formula is 40% cyan, 40% magenta, 40% yellow and 100% black.

Why does this matter? There are certain instances when rich black becomes a significant problem particularly in printed presentations but it does show up in some digital presentations as well. Usually the rich black issue is seen when one black background is adjacent to another black background and the two backgrounds have been generated in different software programs. Basically, one of the blacks will appear blacker than the other. A common and practical example happens between Adobe InDesign and Adobe Photoshop. A model image with a 100% black background (this is an Adobe Photoshop file) placed within a bounding box in Adobe InDesign with a black fill produces a printed file with a visible difference in the blacks. The black in the Adobe Photoshop file appears much darker than the black within the Adobe InDesign bounding box. To fix this you'll need to change the black in the program that is showing a lighter black to a rich black formula—this is typically in Adobe InDesign. Another way to fix the problem is to eliminate the need for multiple backgrounds and simply increase the canvas size in Adobe Photoshop and make it all one black. This creates the entire black background in one program— Adobe Photoshop—and eliminates the need for rich black correction altogether.

Note: a rich black issue will typically not show up until printed. Sometimes it can also be digitally visible when presentations are projected onto screens larger than a computer monitor. Rich black is deceptive in this way! It doesn't show up while you are working on your files, but does show up during the presentation.[22]

designing the presentation narrative

presentation design

There are several different types of presentations that designers can give and they fall into a handful of categories: printed board presentations, digital presentations, in-person presentations and blind presentations. Any presentation can fit into multiple categories. There could be a printed board presentation with a blind review. There could be a board presentation with a digital review. There could be an in-person presentation that is only digital or one that uses only print material. The combinations are endless. There are advantages and disadvantages to each type of presentation; the truth of the matter is that you will likely not have control over what type of presentation you will need to give but working through the material in this section will help you give the most successful presentation possible. Sometimes you will have the choice between a printed presentation and a digital one. Deciding which primary type of presentation to use can be a challenge. See below for simple pros and cons for each presentation type.

Printed Presentation Pros: With a printed presentation since all of the material is printed and pinned up for the review, all of the visual argument is available for jurors to see at all times. This makes it easier to reference back to material from earlier in your argument or to answer specific questions about your ideas if everything is printed and visible to the jurors. This method allows your entire visual argument to be seen at once. The jury will have a better chance of recognizing correlations within your argument if they can see it all at once.

Printed Presentation Cons: Deciding to print all of your visual material can pose challenges related to scale and legibility. You literally can't zoom in on something to see greater detail if it is printed. Take extra care to ensure maximum legibility of all visual representations at the scale they will be used in the presentation. Also, there could be issues regarding legibility and placement on the

Visual Communication for Architects and Designers: constructing the persuasive presentation

wall. Printed material placed too high on the wall or too low on the wall tends to get ignored simply because it is not within natural lines of sight. Keep this in mind when determining where material will be located on the wall.

Digital Presentation Pros: Digital presentations can offer a lot of opportunities to convey your design argument. You can easily include video content, animated diagrams, digital models, and things of the like. You can also go through a lot more material digitally because you don't have to worry about things like issues of pinup space allocations.

Digital Presentation Cons: The reasons for staying away from a digital presentation are all related to the fact that as you move through your slide deck, you are essentially leaving behind all the visual content that you have presented. There is no way for the jury to remember or visually reference previous parts of your presentation. It becomes difficult for the jury to do anything but discuss the last few slides in the presentation. And if they do wish to see something from earlier in the argument, you are stuck with the kludgy method of manually scrolling back through slides to try to find what they are talking about.

Keep in mind these pros and cons for printed and digital presentations. And remember, a combination printed presentation and digital presentation is always an option!

Let's look back at the definition of a presentation narrative from the earlier discussion about how all of the design narratives—presentation narrative, visual narrative and project narrative—work together. The presentation narrative is specifically the order or manner in which the designer wants their project to be understood. The presentation narrative could be demonstrated through a verbal presentation where the designer verbally "narrates" the design argument using the visual material as a reference. Or the presentation narrative could be demonstrated through the order—both through hierarchy relationships and through adjacency relationships—of representational artifacts arranged physically on the presentation boards or in the digital presentation slide deck.

Building a Complex Argument

Design arguments are typically complex arguments that require quite a bit of work to get them organized in a fashion that is easily communicated in a presentation. It is important that the designer spends a significant amount of time trying to achieve clarity regarding the intricate reasoning surrounding design problems. It has already been mentioned that during each project you should keep a running list of design ideas and determine what kind of artifact best represents each idea as you are working through the design process. One of the most important strategies to think about while developing your presentation narrative is determining exactly what you want your review discussion to be centered around. While it is not entirely possible to control how a jury or set of reviewers will respond to your argument; there are ways to subtly guide them toward topics that are relevant to what you would like to discuss.

How many times have you presented a project just to have the jury fixate on one little thing that wasn't even important to the work you've been doing? It happens more often that you'd think! If you want your design jury to discuss ideas around a specific topic, then you need to design the presentation narrative to allow for it. In order to achieve this, make sure to have a hierarchical list of design ideas with requisite artifacts to support these ideas. When determining exactly what will be emphasized, structure the argument such that visual content points back to these specific ideas each time.

When presenting verbally, start with a brief outline of what you will be presenting, repeating the structure of the primary ideas. Then proceed through the visual material always verbalizing exactly how each artifact you discuss supports those primary ideas you outlined in the beginning. Keep in mind when you start talking, the jury is really just settling in and getting oriented to the presentation. They are looking over the visual material and frankly aren't listening just yet. Use this beginning time to slowly introduce what the presentation will be about and give the jury time to start focusing on what's being said. Don't jump in too fast and say the most

Presentation Design—**Designing the Presentation Narrative**

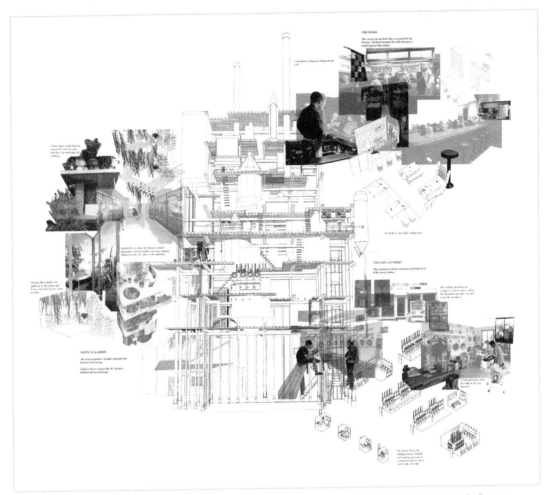

This complex annotated drawing explains activities and spatial requirements through overlaid imagery and axonometric diagrams against the primary section perspective. Drawing selection from Dichotomy of Kyoto by Ayah Hatahet. To review additional work from this project, see page 76.

Visual Communication for Architects and Designers: constructing the persuasive presentation

This drawing collection illustrates that multiple colors are not required for a beautiful and ethereal presentation, Sana Lotus: Derwent Reservoir Hydrotherapy Centre by Dovydas Simkus.

Presentation Design—**Designing the Presentation Narrative**

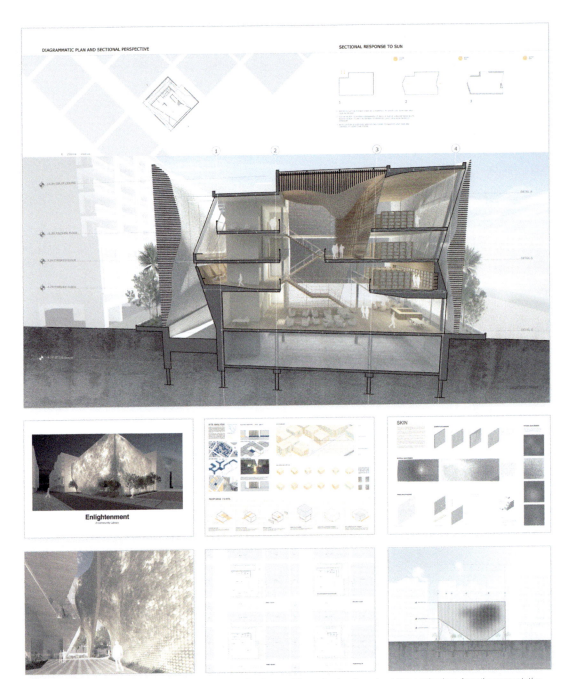

Subtle use of color draws the eye to certain elements while also providing cohesion throughout these selections from the presentation, Enlightenment: A Community Library by Nada Khalaf.

Visual Communication for Architects and Designers: constructing the persuasive presentation

important idea in the first sentence; it will often be missed entirely by the jury. Remember to end the presentation with a little bit of a recap of the primary ideas you would like to center the discussion around. Quite often the jury will discuss the last of what has been presented; not always, but it happens enough to pay attention and try to direct the conclusion of the presentation.

It is also important to remember that in the presentation narrative, the design ideas should be the center of the discussion. Avoid simply reverting to a recitation of your process. It really doesn't matter when you did anything in the design process. The design ideas and overall objectives of the project are what matters in the presentation. Focus on those ideas and avoid even thinking in terms of. . . first I did this, then I did that. Ideas are the most important thing to convey!

In-Person Reviews versus Blind Reviews

There are quite a few fundamental differences when developing a presentation narrative for an in-person review versus a blind review. The most obvious distinction is that for an in-person review the designer is present to guide the discussion while in a blind review, the designer is not present for the presentation and the visual and written content has to carry the entire design argument. It may seem that it is more advantageous to always be present when delivering a design argument but this is not always the case. As mentioned before, sometimes in live juries the design discussion can veer off track. With a blind review—as is often with competitions—the juror typically maintains more concrete attention to the design argument since they have to discover it by themselves. See the section called Strategies for Different Presentation Types for more

Presentation Design—**Designing the Presentation Narrative**

Animated section creates a dialogue between activities and spatial zones in this drawing, Exploring Paradise Square by Catalina Elena Ionita.

detailed information. Just keep in mind that though these presentation types are very different in the delivery of the presentation narrative, the work of the designer should be the same. Just because the designer is present for an in-person review doesn't mean that their design boards shouldn't be structured with clarity and communication in mind.

Printed Boards versus Digital Slide Decks

Presentation narratives for printed boards versus digital slide decks can be quite different. The process to develop primary design ideas and design artifacts to represent those ideas is the same. Hierarchy of design ideas still needs to be established. All of the work to get the project narrative resolved is the same. The real difference comes in structuring the argument.

Using a digital slide deck—often developed in Microsoft PowerPoint or simply as a PDF—forces the designer to work in a very linear fashion by nature of the physical process of moving from one slide to the next. It can become a challenge to only reveal one piece of the argument at a time. However, there are some unique opportunities available when working with digital slide decks. The most obvious one is the ability to build up a design argument by literally building up a drawing or diagram step by step so that the reviewers can systematically understand how certain elements were developed. Knowing that there are opportunities like the one just described while developing the presentation narrative for digital slide decks can change not only how you might be able to talk about an issue but also can change the way you actually create your drawings such that they can be broken down within the presentation.

Visual Communication for Architects and Designers: constructing the persuasive presentation

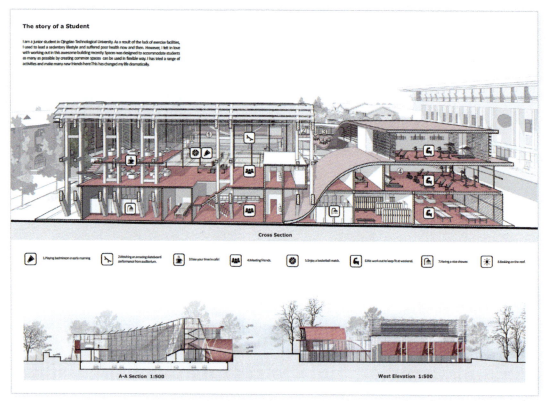

Activity icons are used to transform a section perspective into a fully narrative representation. Drawing selections from Behavior Reflector: Campus Gymnasium by Wei Fan.

right: Consistent use of primary and secondary image hierarchy along with consistent typeface hierarchy, color families and a robust system of call-outs and annotations support the success of this thorough presentation, The Drainage Filter for the Everglades by Qiwei Song, Meikang Li and Chaoyi Cui.

When structuring the presentation narrative for a board layout, the opportunities are quite different from a digital slide deck. With a board layout, all of the content is visible at one time making it easier to see the relationships between artifacts presented on the boards. Adjacencies and groupings are much more important to the structure of the argument and the presentation narrative needs to take this into account. It makes no sense to separate items that need visual adjacency for content communication. With board layout, the designer needs to work diligently to structure the physical arrangement of items on the board to improve the clarity of the message—put like items together and use adjacencies and white space to create packs of visual information to deliver specific messages.

Presentation Design—**Designing the Presentation Narrative**

Visual Communication for Architects and Designers: constructing the persuasive presentation

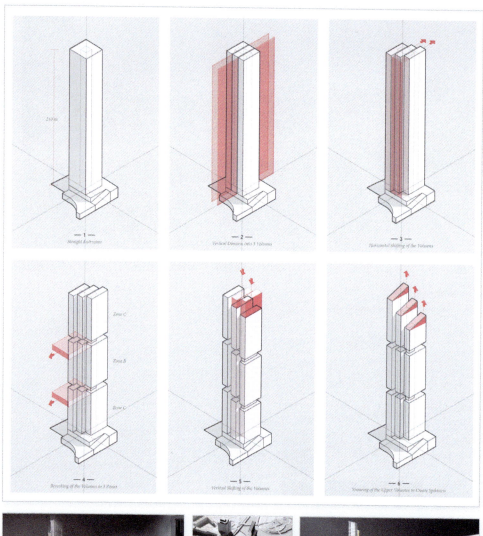

This drawing series shows the power of a step-by-step aggregating diagram in explaining the manipulation of this building form. Drawing and model selections from Reimagining Hamburg's Skyline: a Trades Guild in the HafenCity by Ece Comert and Benjamin Hayes.

Presentation Design—**Designing the Presentation Narrative**

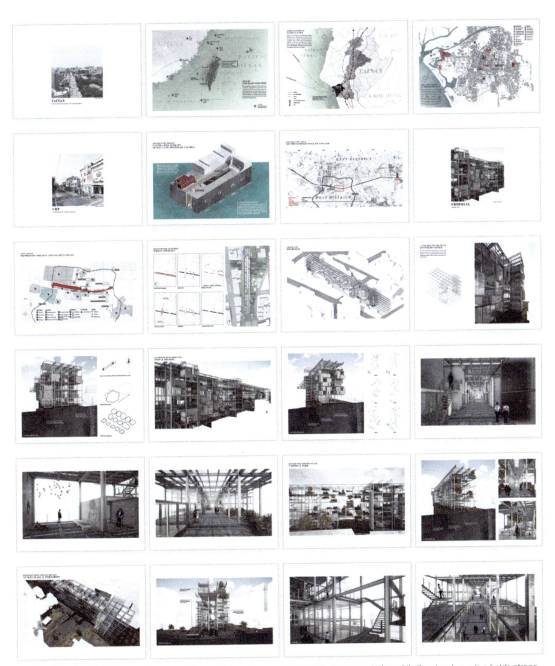

An organized, structural typographic system is used to launch new topics within the presentation while the visual narrative holds strong with large, highly resolved images from Tainan: A City Full of Vitality and Controversy by Kuan Chieh Huang.

designing boards

presentation design

Designing boards seems to be the most common method to present design projects. There are trends that come and go in board layout design but there are also standard board design strategies that will always apply. Keep these basic structural strategies in mind no matter what visual approach is taken with the presentation boards.

Strategies for Board Organization

Presentation boards must always have an organizational strategy in mind. Throughout this book, you will find all sorts of different things to keep in mind when laying out your board and visual argument; all of those ideas still apply—grid and alignment systems, active area and margins, visual relationships of objects on the page, location of primary images, white space and adjacency, visual weight, use of color, and the list goes on and on. All of these principles need to be considered and implemented along with the suggestions for overall board organization found in this section. It is not possible to apply every single recommendation, just be aware of all of the different opportunities to make your visual message clear and apply those that make sense for your work.

Another way to think about things is to completely separate the idea of visual organization and conceptual organization. This method can simply help the designer determine appropriate adjacencies without worrying too much about how things look. For this to work you need to establish organizational groupings based on conceptual meaning. The representations are completely organized around the ideas they support instead of how they look. Then, and only then, start to make decisions about where material should be located on the boards based on how it looks—visual weight, color, etc.

Zone Design

Zone design is an organizational tool that relates to packing information into specific zones on the board. For instance, as the presentation narrative is being developed and content is being developed, create zones where certain types of content will live on the boards once the content is complete. This is easy to describe when thinking about something like diagrams; create a zone on the board where the diagrams will live and think through their organization based on the primary ideas that need to be communicated through diagram. An easy way to begin to organize a board through zone design is to decide if the primary board organization will be vertical columns or horizontal bands. Try to make the content fit one or the other of these orientations and only break the rules when it is absolutely necessary. This strategy is a relatively efficient method to get things immediately organized. Once you understand the primary direction of your board organization, it makes it easier to understand the proportion of individual graphic material that still needs to be produced. With great generality, a vertically oriented board tends to work best with horizontal bands while a horizontally oriented board tends to work best with vertical columns. If there is a choice, select a vertical board and use horizontal banding. We are trained to read things left to right along horizontal lines.

Directional Design: How the Eye Moves Around the Board

Sometimes zone design gets a little bit too normative and the board takes on a completely patterned look, for example, multiple strong horizontal bands can become too visually powerful. This is problematic because once the eye recognizes a strong pattern, it becomes more difficult to see the content over the pattern. If this starts to happen, it is time to start employing directional design strategies. Directional design strategies look specifically at the white space—designed negative space—where there is the absence of content to begin to create spaces of visual pause and movement around the board. These can be completely negative areas—areas that are simply the color of the background or they can be areas of relative openness such as a calm sky in a rendering or the like. The important thing to remember is that with directional design, rather than looking specifically at the organization of content, the designer looks at and designs the negative space between objects and groupings to establish variety of scale for the negative space. This variety of scale of negative space gives the eye areas of respite while traveling around the board taking in the content.

Foreground, Middle Ground and Background

Thus far, the board organization discussions have completely focused on elements as they reside in one plane of the board. An additional organizational

Presentation Design—**Designing Boards**

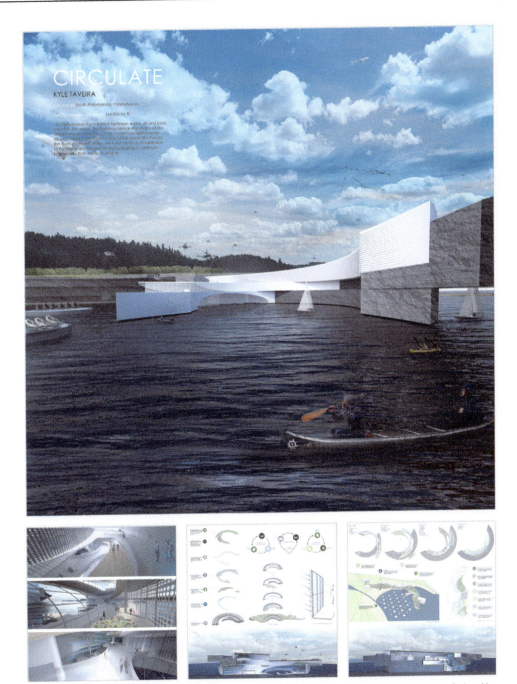

Rendered imagery with rich color tones is primarily organized in horizontal bands while support diagrams are clustered in sub-groups in this presentation, Circulate by Kyle Taveira.

101

Visual Communication for Architects and Designers: constructing the persuasive presentation

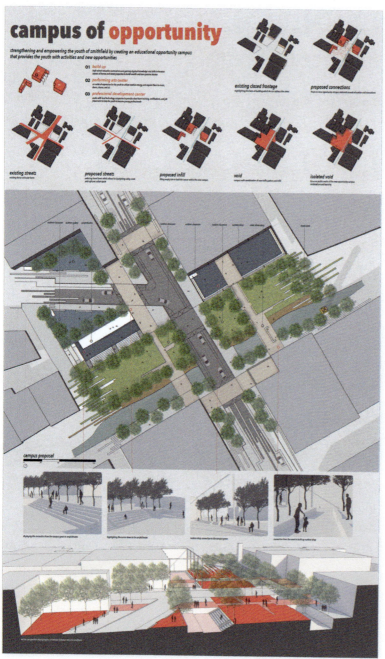

Vignettes are superimposed on the plan drawing elevating them to the foreground in this presentation, Campus of Opportunity by Aaron Neal.

strategy is to design in foreground, middle ground and background planes within the presentation. This design strategy establishes a natural order of importance where the background fades back by design thus visually elevating both the middle ground and the foreground. All issues of zones and graphic strategies still apply but working through these visual fields opens up an extraordinary amount of additional visual space on the board. However, there can be challenges related to getting material to visually lift off the page. Be careful that using layered space on the board does not make it more difficult to read any of the visual content. This organization strategy is not overlapping, it is layering. Overlapping is problematic because multiple pieces of content perceptually remain on the same layer. Working with background, middle ground and foreground specifically strives to move material to different visual levels of planes on the two-dimensional surface. The best way to think about it is to try to objectify the foregrounded objects over the surface of the board. A foregrounded drawing could be encapsulated by a shape that holds it separate from the surface of the board. Changing the scale of the foregrounded material is also helpful. Sometimes adding a very slight drop shadow to the foregrounded object further enhances its foregrounded qualities.

Eye Level Presentation Strategies

There are certain board organization strategies that are specifically related to how exactly a board presentation will be reviewed. If the boards will be reviewed digitally then eye level strategies do not apply. However, if the boards will be pinned up in either an in-person or blind review, then the designer must consider exactly how the boards will be reviewed and make some decisions based on the specific condition of the review.

First let's consider a standing review. This can sometimes be a competition review situation where there are many boards hung together and the jury walks between the boards and reviews the projects while standing. In this case, the designer needs to be very careful about the content placed in the zone of visibility; that is where the eyes naturally rest during review. Average standing eye level, considering both men and

Diagrams and the building section reside in the foreground while the rendered night view is in the background. The lighting of the rendered building illuminates the form and allows for a shift of hierarchy and visual focus between foreground and background. Museum of Contemporary Art by Lauren Wertz.

Visual Communication for Architects and Designers: constructing the persuasive presentation

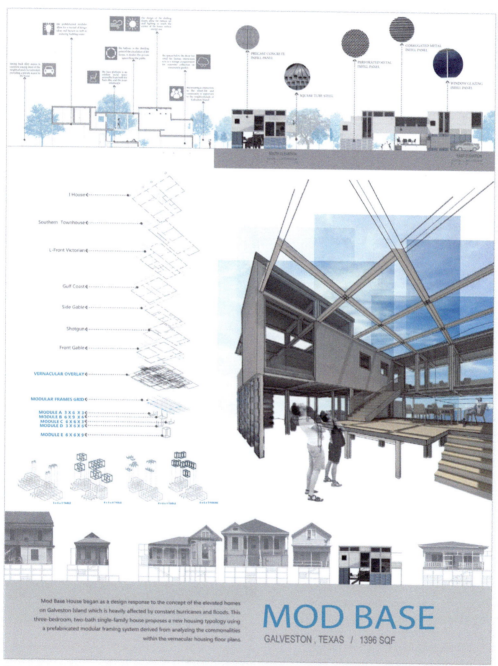

Tones of gray and blue work together to move objects between levels of foreground, middle ground and background. Mod Base by K. Michelle Doll, Jennifer Minor and Kayli Yentzen with Zui Ng.

women of various heights, is at about five feet or one and a half meters. This is where the eye will discover content first. When standing, the most explanatory visual and written content needs to be in a zone near this level. This is where it will be most comfortable for reviewers to focus on content and therefore understand the design argument. Content located above this zone should be large enough and visually powerful enough for reviewers to understand the message of the content without needing to get close to it. Content located at the very bottom of the board needs similar consideration. While it is possible for reviewers to get down on their hands and knees to see detailed material located at the bottom of the board, it is not likely they will do so.

In a seated review, there are similar challenges with slightly different recommendations. It is still true that visual material located at the very top and very bottom of the board or wall needs to be material that can be understood from a distance. However, in a seated review, all content needs to be understood from a distance. The designer can no longer rely on the fact that jurors will stand up and move close enough to drawings to see and understand complex detail. Keep this in mind when designing the presentation narrative for a seated review. Test it with a colleague and see if everything—text included—is visible from a seated location. It is most likely that everything—line weight, color choices, text size—will all need to be bumped up a little so it is visible. Make sure to place the model at the eye level of the seated jurors. It may also be appropriate to have the model simply located on the floor. However, start with it at eye level and place on the floor if requested. No juror wants to be forced to crawl around on the floor; give them a better option.

This elongated rendering anchors the board and through a gradient of color allows room for detailed content above. Perceiving Sensation by Matthew Wieber.

Visual Communication for Architects and Designers: constructing the persuasive presentation

Common Board Challenges

There are a handful of things that can be universally demanding when developing a board layout. Luckily there are only two fundamentally difficult issues. These design issues are dealing with assigned board proportions and how to manage visual content jumping the gap between boards. The other challenges mentioned here are much easier to control and resolve.

Dealing with Assigned Board Proportions
Usually the size, proportion and orientation of presentation boards are established ahead of time and cannot be altered by the designer. This can pose quite a problem because each designer's project will naturally develop different graphic material in a wide variety of proportions. Vertical boards tend to work the best for reasons we've already discussed. When you find yourself with a significantly horizontal board, see if it is possible to split it into two vertical boards that can be designed to be adjacent. Thinking this way may help figure out zone strategies. Of course, if your content is primarily horizontal, a horizontal board will work best! Square boards are particularly challenging but are used quite frequently for design competitions. It is best to try to break the natural symmetry found in the square to get more flexibility within the layout. It is perfectly fine to use one large image for a square board, even though that is technically a symmetrical layout. However, avoid a four-square grid of images; this will put the visual focus on the center white space crossing

Presentation Design—**Designing Boards**

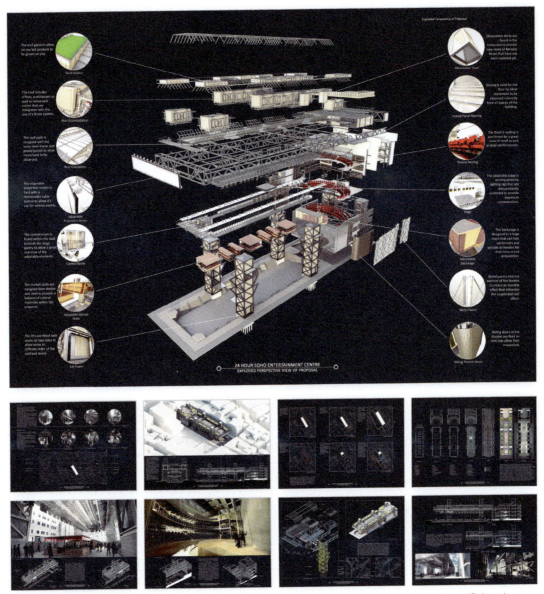

above and left: The lower horizontal band on these boards is used where necessary to organize content on each specific board as well as across all boards. The vertical alignment of the circle forms of these call-outs organizes the shapes so they can convey detailed information without becoming visually distracting. 24 Hour Soho Entertainment Centre by Andrei-Ciprian Cojocaru.

Visual Communication for Architects and Designers: constructing the persuasive presentation

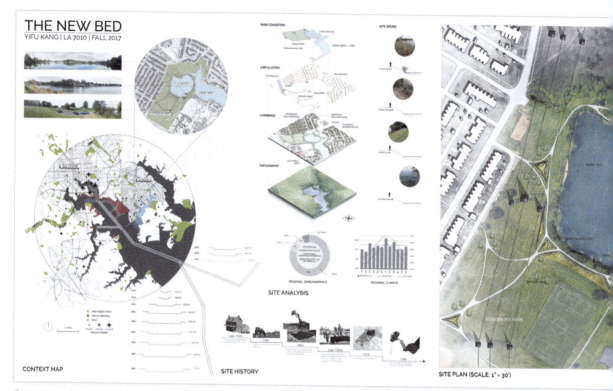

Content groupings, drawings at multiple scales and the effective use of foreground, middle ground and background allow for ample information without visual clutter. Organizing similar material into vertical columns also helps with content organization. The New Bed by Yifu Kang.

of margins. Instead, really work with visual hierarchy to create a natural viewing order starting with the largest and most visually prominent image and working through hierarchical groupings of ideas to explain secondary and tertiary content.

Jumping the Gap

When you have multiple boards in a presentation, inevitably the designer will be faced with the issue of the gap between the sheets of the layouts. Sometimes this situation is created simply by the requirements of the project deliverables and sometimes this situation is created due to a discrepancy between plotter dimensions and final board dimensions. In the latter case, the board layout needs to be split into printable sheets that fit in the plotter. It really doesn't matter if you need to spread an image across multiple boards; if you need to do it, then you need to do it. However, there are some best practices to consider before doing so. If you do jump an image across multiple boards, make sure that the split between the boards does not happen at a critical location within a complex drawing. Also make sure when plotting the boards that you plot a little bit of overlap on each board so that when the boards are trimmed you can ensure an exact alignment.

Horizontal or Vertical Components of Board Layout

Frequently a project design will have elements that are predominantly horizontal or predominantly vertical. Don't let this be a disturbance to the development of the board layout. Depending on the site and context of

Presentation Design—**Designing Boards**

SECTION ELEVATION + SYSTEM DIAGRAM

a project, there could be some really strange drawing proportions and orientations. Roll with it and remember the guidelines about setting up zone organization for the board. Let the organization be what it needs to be. However, make sure to take a moment to review whether or not the primary orientation of the content is driving the board layout into a condition where the legibility of the pattern is overtaking the legibility of the content. If this happens, adjustments will need to be made to pull the board layout out of this orientation trap.

Graphic Challenges of Shaped Diagrams

There is a visual trend of pulling secondary or support content off the visual plane of the board by placing them within a circle or a soft square. This can be a very effective strategy to achieve clear layers on the board and separate different types of content from others. Be careful, however, that the shape of the diagram doesn't become so visually prominent that is distracts from the actual legibility of the content. Periodically pin the boards up and step back and make sure the shapes are not too powerful. If they are, consider changing shapes, reducing line weights, color strength, or even opacity of the entire object. It is a constant effort of moving back and forth to work out appropriate layers of foreground, middle ground and background on a layout.

109

Setup and Submission

Adobe InDesign Board Setup Tips and Tricks

When laying out multiple boards in Adobe InDesign, it is best to set the files up so that all of the boards are in the arrangement that they will be presented when pinned up. This way, the designer can see all of the spatial, grouping and alignment relationships between boards as they will actually be when presented. If the boards are set up as single pages and not viewed together, it can be quite difficult to capitalize on alignment relationships across boards as the layout is being developed. Once it is time to print, separate the boards into individual pages in Adobe InDesign and print.

If the assigned board size is larger than the maximum width permitted on the plotter, then create the Adobe InDesign file as one large board when designing so that all alignments and relationships are clear. Then when time to print, group everything in Adobe InDesign and copy to the correct size page for plotting, shifting the grouped content as needed to get the correct material plotted on each page.

Paper Selection and Ink Saturation

Different paper finishes produce vastly different image results. Presentations should be tested on both coated and uncoated paper to determine which gives the best result for image clarity. Coated paper is treated with a sealant-like coating that changes the way the paper accepts and absorbs ink. Coated paper typically comes in a range of gloss, satin and matte. Be mindful when selecting high gloss paper, sometimes the reflection of light on the paper makes it more difficult to see the visual material on the board. Also be aware that matte paper for a plotter often has a minimal coating and therefore it still absorbs quite a lot of ink. Uncoated papers that have no sealant on the surface completely absorb the ink into the paper. Uncoated papers tend to dull printed colors significantly. Satin paper is a reasonable compromise between gloss paper and matte paper. Typically, when comparing print quality and paper surface for plotter paper, satin coated looks the best. The surface of the paper holds the ink and does not let it get absorbed and dulled. This paper is also not so shiny as to cause a glare when viewing. However, since paper finishes and print quality vary between different paper manufacturers, the bottom line is to test, test, test.

There can be a lot of cost associated with these test plots on expensive paper. If this is the case, digitally create narrow strips of content that cut through important graphic pieces of your argument and set up a separate Adobe InDesign plot file that just has these strips that you can then print on a smaller piece of the nicer paper. This way you can test color, line weight, hierarchy, etc. without having to print full boards each time.

What Software to Use and Why

Printed or projected presentations should be designed in graphic layout software such as Adobe InDesign or similar. Use programs such as Adobe Photoshop for editing image raster files (pixel-based), Adobe Illustrator for vector (line and tone) drawings and Microsoft Word for text information. Using each piece of software for the reason it was designed not only makes sense, it will also make your design life much easier.

Adobe InDesign works seamlessly to connect with other Adobe programs like Photoshop and Illustrator by linking them into a layout program. Basically, you can set up Adobe InDesign to the size and proportion of your layout and link drawings and images you have generated in the other programs. Since the drawings and images are linked to the Adobe InDesign layout file and not embedded, each time you make an edit to the drawing or image files, they are updated in the layout.

Since Adobe Photoshop is a raster-based program—it is driven by pixel-based images—no text or drawing line work should be done in Adobe Photoshop. It is quite difficult to scale material generated in a raster program because the files are limited regarding scalability to its initial resolution as defined by pixels per inch. Once a digital image is created, the relationship between pixels and the size of the image remains in a relative and proportional relationship for the life of the image. The physical size of the image can be adjusted or the number of pixels per inch can be adjusted; but since

Presentation Design—Designing Boards

these two numbers work proportionately together, if one is adjusted, the other is automatically adjusted. You cannot add pixels to a raster file and increase its resolution and thus its size. If a raster image is scaled beyond its resolution, it will appear pixelated.

Adobe Illustrator is a vector-based program, and as such, graphic material drawn in Adobe Illustrator is infinitely scalable. Vector graphics are calculated using mathematics to define points and lines. Since vector graphics are not defined by pixels, they can be scaled without resolution issues; they will not lose image quality as raster files do when scaled. Adobe Illustrator should be used for all line drawings so that they can be scaled as needed for board layout. If orthographic drawings were created in AutoCAD, these .dwgs files can be converted to Adobe Illustrator files. Adobe Illustrator has more flexible editing tools for presentation drawing needs.

Though text is technically a vector graphic and can be scaled, it is best to write in a program similar to Microsoft Word so that you can take full advantage of the editing capabilities of that software. Once a solid draft is completed, this text can be placed and edited further in Adobe InDesign. Placing text in Adobe InDesign makes it infinitely easier to edit than if it were in Adobe Illustrator or Adobe Photoshop since there are no issues of scale adjustment to consider. Think of this, if text—even for a diagram title—is in Adobe Illustrator, when that diagram is placed in the Adobe InDesign board layout file it will likely be scaled to adjust to the layout. When the diagram is scaled, if the text is in Adobe Illustrator it will also be scaled. All of a sudden, across a series of diagrams, there is a variety of sizes to the diagram labels. Bottom line, put all presentation text in the board layout file in Adobe InDesign.

Digital Submission of Boards

Usually when submitting boards digitally, a PDF is required. There are certain methods and strategies to get the best quality file and the smallest size. Often competition submissions will require a PDF that is within a restricted file size. This can be a challenge. Be very careful that the file optimization of the PDF does not reduce the quality of the visual content such that it is no longer clear and legible.

Exporting a PDF from Adobe InDesign

There are several methods to export a PDF from Adobe InDesign. One particular method is recognized by most printing services and publishers as the preferred method to achieve the best results. This is the process: in Adobe InDesign navigate to the top menu bar, select File / Adobe PDF Presets / High Quality Print. The pop-up menu will then provide a range of options: compression settings, crop marks, bleed settings, etc. Output at maximum resolution—no less than a downsampling to 300 pixels per inch—to maintain maximum quality. It is best to output at a maximum quality from Adobe InDesign and then to work through the PDF optimization processes to reduce file size while keeping an eye on image quality. See below for PDF optimization strategies.

Optimizing PDF Files: How to Manage Resolution and PDF Output

One of the most challenging things about outputting a presentation as a PDF is managing image quality versus file size. Often when submitting presentations digitally, there is quite a small file size requirement. Once a PDF is exported by the High Quality Print method as described above, the resultant file size can often be too big to be practical and useful. There is a fine balance between adjusting the output quality of the images and the resultant file size. Reduce the PDF file size so that the file can be emailed or uploaded but make sure not to sacrifice image quality in the process of optimization. There are some tricks.

To optimize a PDF file, do the following: open the PDF in Adobe Acrobat Pro; select File / Save As or Save As Other / Optimized PDF; in the pop-up window under Image Settings, ensure that all ppi settings are below 300ppi; select Discard User Data in the left window; select Discard Private Data of Other Applications; select Discard Hidden Layer Content and Flatten Visible Layers in the main window. Click OK.

Determine what the required file size limitations are for a PDF submission—this will be provided by the organization being submitted to—and work toward those specifications.

Visual Communication for Architects and Designers: constructing the persuasive presentation

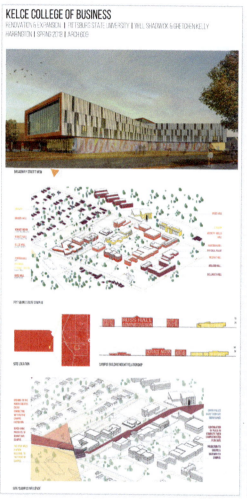
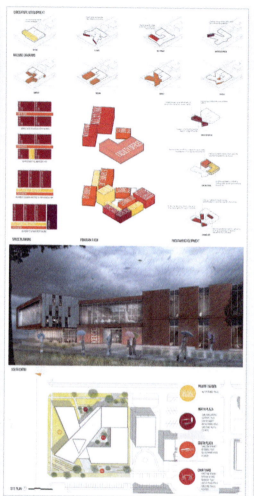

Presentation Design—**Designing Boards**

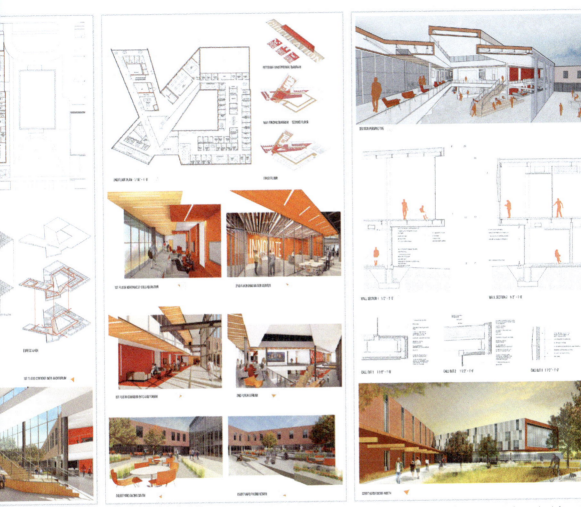

Unifying colors and sub-sets of diagram information work together to organize an extraordinary amount of complex information in this presentation, Kelce College of Business by Gretchen Kelly and Will Shadwick.

113

text in your presentation: content and visual goals

presentation design

The correct and strategic inclusion of thoughtful and specific text in your presentation is critical to the success of the delivery of your design argument. The textual argument should be developed as the visual presentation is being developed. Remember all of the work described earlier in this publication about the development of the project and presentation narrative where lists were generated of primary design ideas and the artifacts that support them? This written list can and should form the basis for your written argument and should appear within your presentation. Do not put dummy text—text that you intend to replace with "real" text—into the presentation. Always attempt to write the argument. Time and iteration is needed to revise drawn representations; the same is true for written arguments.

Including text in your presentation can achieve both visual goals and verbal goals toward ultimately conveying the design thinking and meaning behind your work. Do not short change the potential of your presentation by leaving this work until the end. By then, it will be too late and the delivery of your argument will be significantly diminished. Only when you understand the value of the words selected for your design argument, will you come to understand the purpose they serve in your presentation.

When you are in a live review—one that you are actively participating in, as opposed to a blind review—text elements within your presentation can be extremely helpful as verbal cues referencing what you intend to say during the presentation. One of the greatest fears of live presentations is getting up in front of your jury of reviewers and going blank, completely forgetting what the design argument is and what is important to say. Use the text on the boards as visual triggers to help remember what should be said. Blanking out during a presentation happens; be prepared!

Bottom line: text descriptions should be developed alongside the visual representations that are defining your work. And remember, text selection greatly impacts a reviewer's understanding of your work. This is completely within your control. Selecting and implementing specific words can alter the manner in which the work is seen and reviewed. And remember when a project is presented, this is the designer's opportunity to convey their specific goals and objectives studied through the work. Relying on words developed by others (your instructor, classmates, colleagues, etc.) completely eliminates your own voice.

Leaving text and argument development until the end of the project or, even worse, until the end of the presentation design completely limits your ability to convey the message behind your work. Strive to resolve the message during the design process so that it is apparent what should be conveyed to the reviewer. Then spend energy making sure that message actually gets delivered.

There are different types of text that need to be included within a presentation to fully describe a project and aid in the conveyance of the design argument. At least the following should be included:

Project Title / Subtitle

Project Statistics: this could be project location, size, type, credits, etc.

Descriptive Body Text

Captions

Drawing and Diagram Titles

Drawing and Diagram Labels[1]

Three Levels of Visual Reading of a Presentation

With presentations, it is not always possible to be present in person for the review; these are typically referred to as blind reviews. Since the designer is not present, the presentation alone has to do all of the communication work to convey to the reviewers what is specifically important for them to understand about a project. Do not rely on large paragraphs of descriptive text to convey all of the ideas; this text rarely gets thoroughly read during a presentation review.

During a blind review, as in an architectural competition, reviewers have a lot of projects to review—sometimes hundreds! It is important to understand that when reviewing such large numbers of presentations with the goal of selecting a handful of winners, reviewers will not be reading and studying each presentation with the depth and detail that the designer desires. Generally, competition presentation reviews will follow a three-tiered approach to reviewing the projects, all in an effort to get down to a set of projects that will be considered finalists in the competition.

1. High-level browsing: this is typically a very quick review of the presentation boards. The reviewer is looking for high-level design arguments as well as design and representation skill. In order to move forward in a design competition, the presentation must make it past this phase.

2. Mid-level browsing: this is a slower review of a presentation. During this type of review, the reviewer is likely going back through all of the presentations after the high-level browse generated a "look at this again" list for the projects. With this pass, the reviewer is looking for full project information and is reading fragments of easily accessible text. The goal for this type of review is to gain a better understanding of the correlation between ideas and the visual representation of those ideas. The reviewer will read things like project statistics, captions, diagram labels, etc.

3. In-depth review: this is the complete, take your time and really understand everything review. For this level of presentation review, the reviewer looks at everything in the presentation and attempts to stitch together the entire design argument through written text and representative imagery. If your project presentation has made it to this stage, it is likely that the reviewer is also looking for clarity in design argument so that they, themselves, can argue the project into the finals of the competition. Giving them critical and key words to use, through captions, labels and descriptive text is helpful!

Keep these three levels of the visual reading of a presentation in mind when developing text strategies to convey your design ideas and make sure that the design argument can be detected through all three levels of review. And keep in mind, even though these three levels of reading were discussed through the lens of a blind review, these principles apply to all presentation types.[2]

What it Says: The Value of Words

Take care with the selection of words for your design argument. Besides having meaning, words have value. Their worth can be measured in their ability to communicate. Using words superfluous to your message is counterproductive. The more concise and precise the word selection, the clearer the message. Additionally, don't leave text out and assume the intent is obvious through drawings and images. Important ideas will be lost!

Project Titles and Subtitles

Assign project titles and subtitles based on what the audience should know about your specific design approach to the project rather than what the project has been titled through official means—competition title, course title, etc. This is an important opportunity to give the reviewers the lens through which they should be evaluating the project.

Project Statistics

Project statistics provide a one-look, easy to understand synopsis of the program type and breadth of a project. Typical categories included in a project statistics list are: project type, location, size, date of completion, role, etc. Anything that can be clearly conveyed in a short list should be included here.

Project Descriptive Text

Project descriptive text is just as it sounds and is the one place within the presentation where the full design argument should be discussed. Review primary design ideas from the lists that have been developing over the course of the project and organize the written argument in the order of importance of the design ideas. Keep in mind that not every reviewer will read this entire text so be careful with your word choice and be clear and concise. If a project statistics list has been included—project type, location, size, date of completion, role, etc.—it is not necessary to repeat any of this information in the descriptive text. Use this to your advantage and concentrate on the direct conveyance of the design ideas.

Captions, Drawing and Diagram Titles and Labels

Captions, drawing and diagram titles and labels by their very nature are brief and concise pieces of text. Because of this, it is really important that each and every word has an incredible amount of value and ability to convey meaning. Write these captions, drawing and diagram titles and labels to direct the reviewer to exactly what they should see in the project imagery and what framework they should use to review the project.

Simple Strategies for the Written and Verbal Development of Your Argument

Developing both a written argument and a verbal argument for your design project is a must. While these two types of arguments seem similar, they are actually two very different types of arguments. Both arguments need to be concise, but the written argument relies more on the value of words simply because there is no way to force a reviewer to read absolutely everything in the presentation. Consequently, the more succinct the written argument can be, the better. The verbal argument—the actual words that will be said during a presentation—is a particular challenge. It is a different exercise to write an argument concisely on the presentation than to verbally lead the jurors through a complex yet concise design argument. Keep these differences in mind while you are structuring both arguments.

It is important to be purposeful regarding the writing style in a presentation; it says a lot about what the designer thinks about his or her own work. Keep these writing tips in mind while cultivating both the written and verbal argument for your presentation:

Visual Communication for Architects and Designers: constructing the persuasive presentation

1. Write first, edit second. At first, don't worry about grammar, spelling, order of ideas, appropriateness of ideas, etc. Just write. There will be time as the design work progresses to hone and refine the words associated with it. It is always a good strategy to capture all ideas by writing them down. If you don't write them down, they simply do not exist! Waiting for words and ideas come out fully formed is like sitting and waiting for an entire architectural design to form in your mind before trying to draw it or build it. It just doesn't work that way. Words operate the same way.

2. Write when in a good mood. Don't write when exhausted. Figure out what time of the day works best for you to be clear-minded and productive. Write during this time. Also, remember that you don't need to spend a lot of time during your productive time writing; this is also a good time for designing. Just write enough to get the basic ideas down.

3. Avoid the first person. Don't say, "I did this, then this, then this, etc."

4. A simple chronological narrative of the design process is important to have. Keep a running list of what you did when. However, this chronological narrative is not necessarily what should be used to present the project through the presentation narrative.

5. Write about the ideas behind the work, not about yourself or the process. In fact, when writing about your work try to completely eliminate yourself from the equation by looking at the work as if an outsider. . . as if you've never seen it before.

6. It's much easier to identify errors in print so always edit with a printed copy.

7. There should be absolutely no spelling, punctuation or grammar errors in your final text.

8. Keep it simple, clear and concise. There is no need for convoluted language; all it will do is distract the reviewer.

9. Consider the writing to be a design project and treat it as such.

Organizing Your Ideas

Try organizing your cohesive argument several times while developing the project. It is actually harder than you think. Sometimes it is helpful to pose a series of questions to yourself that you must answer. Here are some ideas of useful questions to answer when trying to figure out what your project is actually about:

Questions About Ideas—Thesis
1. What is this project about? Use a four-word phrase, maximum.

2. What does this thesis really mean? Describe it in more detail without using the phrase developed above.

3. I find this an interesting architectural question to study because:

4. I am studying this architectural idea in these ways—or the thesis is specifically studied through these conditions:

5. I selected those situations—or ideas or moments—to study this architectural idea because:

Questions About the Building Program
6. The program of the building is—give it a name and then break it down:

7. I determined this program because—or why this program makes sense for this location:

8. My specific project's response to the overall project design goals is:

Questions About Specific Project Devices (in this example using light)
9. The project's attitude toward light is:

10. The project's attitude toward light is demonstrated in these ways—or the project's attitude toward light was studied in these locations:

11. These are important areas of study because:

12. The project uses these types of light:

13. How does this project demonstrate these types of light?

Questions About Context
14. The project's response to its context is:

15. The project's response to its context is demonstrated in these ways:

Questions About Project Ideas

16. The primary ideas about this project that need to be described both verbally and visually are—or what is everything you want to make sure is said about your project? Make this a concise list.

For additional strategies regarding verbal presentations, see the section on In-Person Presentations.

How it Looks: The Graphic Presence of Text in Your Presentation

We have discussed the value of words and the importance of their careful selection to convey the design thinking behind a project. How the text looks in a presentation is equally important to what it says. Properly selected, placed and designed text creates a certain harmony and visual correctness. Getting the graphic presence of text visually correct can make the difference between a beautiful and credible visual argument and a completely unprofessional effort. Always select a professional and legible typeface, resist the urge to select a trendy or overly stylized typeface.

Fortunately, there are a handful of guidelines to follow that will make typeface decisions deliberate instead of happenstance. These are the guidelines to keep in mind when working through typeface decisions:

1. Select serif or sans serif based solely on legibility factors—see the typeface section in Basics of Graphic Design as Related to Presentations for additional information on this topic. Do not select typefaces based on a perception of style; legibility is the most important thing that matters when selecting typefaces.

2. Choose a typeface that has a broad hierarchical range. Select a typeface that has, at a minimum, bold, medium and light weights. If there is an extended range beyond this, consider it a bonus. If you find yourself with a slightly limited typeface range, you can extend the range by including values of gray as well as black text. Be careful and don't use too many shades of gray; it will add a layer of visual confusion. Limit this typeface range extension to just one or two gradations of gray in addition to black.

3. Make justification decisions also based on the legibility of the text. Do not default automatically to fully justified text right and left because it aligns neatly with the underlying presentation grid. The rivers that tend to show up in fully justified text are very distracting. Left justified text is the most legible. It creates a white space variance at the right edge which can be used to alter the edge away from an overpowering grid. Avoid center justification; it is very difficult to read.

4. Establish a typeface hierarchy system and use it.

Typeface Hierarchy Systems

It is important to establish a visual hierarchy within the typeface selection. This typeface hierarchy works to establish areas of primary focus within the presentation as well as areas of visual support. Keep in mind that typeface selection and use should support the visual images and should not overwhelm the content graphics. Follow this list as guidance for typeface hierarchy. These types of text are organized from most visually prominent to least visually prominent:

1. Project Title

2. Project Subtitle

3. Descriptive Body text

4. Captions

5. Drawing or diagram labels, drawing or diagram titles and call-outs

Remember, typeface hierarchy is not solely related to what piece of text is larger or bolder than others. Visual hierarchy is determined by what pieces of text pull the eye in the strongest way or what holds the most visual prominence on the page. This visual prominence can be achieved in a variety of ways—color, style, weight, etc.

Flexibility Within the Relationships of the Typeface Hierarchy System

It is possible to deviate from the above listed system but be careful not to stray too far or there won't be a framework to work within. This hierarchical system is flexible enough to allow for some changes but there are some hierarchical relationships that should stay correct to the original list.

Visual Communication for Architects and Designers: constructing the persuasive presentation

The title needs to be the most important visual piece of text on a project presentation. It directs the reviewer to the correct subject matter—basically the primary objective of the design project. However, this doesn't mean that the title is necessarily biggest or boldest or in an outrageous typeface. The title should just be prominent enough to gently pull the eye to it when reviewing the presentation.

The relationship between the title and the subtitle has quite a bit of flexibility. The recommended relationship is that the subtitle is subordinate to the title yet still dominant over other text types in the presentation. The subtitle delivers a secondary message about the project and is important enough to not get visually buried in the descriptive body text so it definitely needs visual legibility through separation. However, it is not as significant as the title and therefore should not be as visually prominent. The subtitle should be smaller than the title and clearly different than the body text.

The visual relationship between descriptive body text and caption is an important one to get correct. The body text should be more visually prominent—in this instance it really is a case of it needing to be larger. The body text needs to read as the most important visual block of text within the presentation—it contains the synopsis of the design argument. The caption style must be visually less prominent than the body text, and the difference needs to be significant enough that there is no chance for visual confusion between the style of the body text and the caption text.

The caption text and the diagram label text can be the same size and style if necessary. However, there needs to be a slight adjustment to the hierarchy for drawing and diagram titles. These might be the same size as the caption text and diagram label text but perhaps in bold or italics or perhaps all caps. As mentioned before, do not underline—it is visually distracting.

above and left: Proper balance between the visual hierarchy of the project title and the primary image draws the eye first to the image and then to the title and balances with the remaining text and imagery. Polar Umbrella by Derek Pirozzi.

Typeface to Layout: Balance of Graphic Hierarchy between Image and Text

Each type of text element—title, subtitle, descriptive body text, caption, drawing or diagram labels, drawing or diagram titles, drawing or diagram call-outs—takes up visual space in the presentation and needs to be managed so the visual narrative being told through the project representations remains the primary focus of the reviewer. The best method to keep this relationship true is to make sure that the established typeface hierarchy does not visually compete with any of the graphic material in the presentation. Simple "squint tests" can determine if something is getting out of balance.

Adjacency relationships are an important way to balance the graphic hierarchy between image and text on a page layout. There are several basic adjacency rules to keep in mind:

1. Descriptive body text can float on the board and fill a visual hole. It can act as a stand-alone physical item to visually balance image placement. Remember, left justified text is best for text blocks; just manage the rag right edge of the block so that it doesn't get out of hand with too many hyphens or too many differences between the length of each line.

2. Captions must be adjacent to the image or drawing they reference. Never let a caption visually float too far away from its object without a clear visual reference. A poorly placed caption creates a visual object in its own right on the layout and this can be very distracting. The visual goal for the support text is to be complementary to the image or drawing it is describing; do not let it float away from the object it is supporting.

3. The same attachment rule guides drawing or diagram titles, labels and call-outs; do not let these text types stray too far physically from the visual representation they are titling, labeling or calling out.

Content and Visual Goals of Text in Your Presentation

All of the many types of text in a presentation—title, subtitle, descriptive body text, caption, drawing or diagram labels, drawing or diagram titles, drawing or diagram call-outs—have different content and visual goals relative to the legibility of the project as well as within the legibility of the systems of the entire presentation.

Let's look at the differences and similarities regarding the content and visual goals for these text types. Keep these ideals in mind when designing your presentation narrative, your visual narrative and your project narrative with the ultimate goal of clearly conveying your design thinking argument.

Titles

Content Goal: The content goal of each project title is to direct the reviewer to the primary design objectives for the project in the presentation.

Visual Goal: The visual goal of the project title is to establish a visual starting point within a full presentation of artifacts. It acts as an orienting device to the project ideas within the presentation.

Subtitles

Content Goal: The content goal of the subtitle is to support the content goal of the title with supplementary subordinate information. This information could be any variety of things but should really answer the question, "What is the second most important idea to convey about the project?"

Visual Goal: The visual goal of the subtitle is to create a typeface cushion between the title and adjacent objects on the presentation board. The subtitle also visually acts as a support for the title.

Descriptive Body Text

Content Goal: The content goal of descriptive body text is to convey, as clearly and concisely as possible, the main objectives of the project. This text should be written from your point of view and should not just be a repeat of the assigned project brief. Take this opportunity to use your own voice to convey exactly what you think is important to understand. Keep in mind that this body of text does not always get read. Keep it compelling but simple.

Visual Goal: Descriptive body text takes on a bit of an unusual visual role within the presentation. Its mere presence declares there is substance to a project. Descriptive body text might not always get read but without it a project appears to have less thought behind it. This text block can also provide a series of physical edges—since it takes up substantive physical space on the board—to use in aligning with other visual material within the layout.

Captions

Content Goal: The caption acts as the single most powerful focusing device for each specific image, drawing or diagram. Take advantage of this. The caption, if written correctly, tells the reviewer exactly what to focus on in a representational artifact and reinforces and supports the communication of the project and presentation narrative.

Visual Goal: The visual goal of a caption is to lend visual credence to the image it is supporting simply by existing. An image without a caption appears to have less value simply because it was not even worth the effort to caption.

Drawing or Diagram Titles

Content Goal: Drawing and diagram titles simply announce the purpose of the drawing or diagram. Don't assume, even if the drawing or diagram is a normative one, that the reviewer will understand the significance of its inclusion. Tell them the importance of the drawing or diagram by properly titling it.

Visual Goal: The visual goal of drawing or diagram titles has to do with a fine-grained text resolution on the page. Placing a small collection of words in grounding locations gives the eye a place to rest and then visually enter the drawing or diagram.

Drawing or Diagram Labels and Call-Outs

Content Goal: Drawing and diagram labels and call-outs are vital for the understanding of this type of representation. They provide a secondary layer of

Presentation Design—**Text in Your Presentation: Content and Visual Goals**

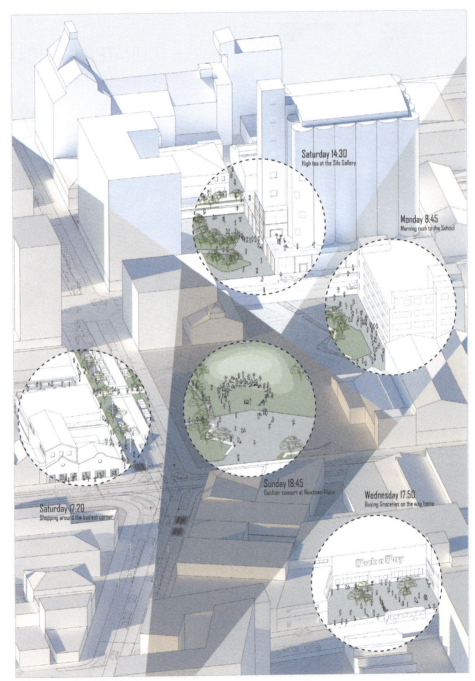

Hierarchical text supports visual call-outs in this time and activity drawing aimed at describing the social and cultural opportunities in this district of Johannesburg, South Africa. Live & Create in Joburg by Shuailin Wu.

Visual Communication for Architects and Designers: constructing the persuasive presentation

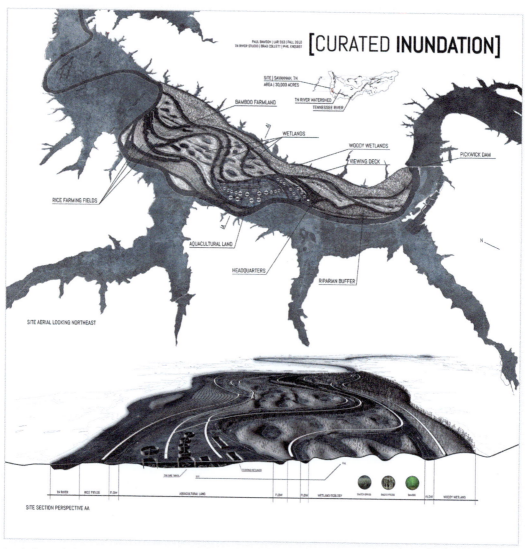

Leader lines pointing to multiple instances of the same call-out are drawn from a single point and then arrayed to reach numerous areas on the drawing. This is a very clean and elegant solution for multiple call-out locations. Curated Inundation by Paul Bamson.

Presentation Design—**Text in Your Presentation: Content and Visual Goals**

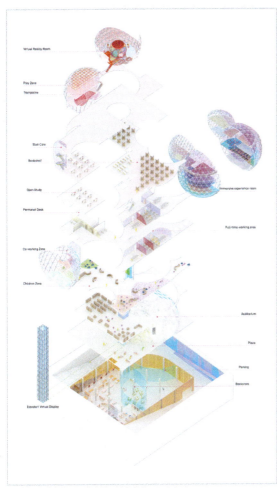

Written call-outs placed above dotted leader lines organize the textual information in a clear way and allow the drawing to be the primary focus. Drawing selection from Library of Co-Existing by Jiaoyue Zhao and Kaiying Lin.

information that is required to understand some of the nuances of a design project. They are each a little different in content and so should be discussed separately.

Drawing labels refer to items such as program labels in a plan drawing. It is imperative that some indication is given in the plan drawings of at least significant programmatic elements, particularly as they relate to the project narrative. It is not necessary to label all programmatic elements; things like mechanical spaces, bathrooms, etc. can be omitted from the drawing program labels. Typically, this type of space is legible just from the fixtures drawn or the scale of the space and therefore no label is needed. Exactly what needs to be labeled should be determined on a case-by-case basis and should be decided not only based on message delivery but also based on the physical space available. Diagram labels are different than something like a program label on a plan drawing in that they often convey a very particular kind of information. Diagram labels can very concisely convey project operations or concise project objectives and should be worded very carefully. A significant amount of substance can come from the words in diagram labels—take the time to construct them deliberately.

There are several universal styles of diagrams that reviewers assume to mean a certain thing. However, there are very nuanced modifications to these types of drawings that can radically change their reading. Be sure to make the specifics of your particular diagrams clear in the labels and /or the call-outs.

Call-outs are small fragments of text that are attached to a drawing or diagram through the use of leader lines. This type of text provides more nuance to the objectives of each representational artifact. They should be used to directly explain specific elements of a drawing or diagram. Since they are attached to a leader line and point directly to the element they are referencing, these call-outs are a great way to convey very detailed information.

Visual Goal: Visually, drawing labels, diagram labels and call-outs all perform similar goals as drawing or diagram titles; they provide visually grounded locations within the layout to help the eye move in and around a drawing or diagram.[3]

strategies for different presentation types

presentation design

There are different presentation strategies for different types of presentations. As we've already discussed, presentations fall into a handful of categories; printed board presentations, digital presentations, in-person presentations and blind presentations. Presentations can also fit into multiple categories. This section aims to identify specific challenges to each type of presentation. When your presentation falls into multiple categories, work through all of these challenges to hone your direction when preparing the presentation.

Combining print and digital presentations can be a great way to leverage the advantages of each type of presentation. Print out visual material that is key to the primary messages of the design argument and that needs to be referenced again and again. Use digital media to support design arguments through sequentially assembled digital diagrams, the linear progression of the message as well as with animations and video content.

In-Person Presentations

In-person presentations have their own specific challenges because in a lot of ways they often rely too much on the person giving the presentation. This can generate quite a bit of stress around the presentation especially for people who do not enjoy public speaking. Even seasoned speakers feel some stress around a verbal presentation. Fortunately, there are some strategies to make this a less taxing experience.

Often it will be a requirement of the presentation to present the argument of the project in a very short amount of time. The fact of the matter is that even a short amount of time feels like an eternity if you are not prepared. When organizing your verbal presentation, make sure to state up front what you are going to argue. Go ahead and lay out the structure of your presentation so the jury can get the framework in mind and listen for the sections of the argument you have outlined. This will reinforce your ideas and ultimately aid in the delivery of your message; you'll essentially say it twice—first as an outline and then with more elaboration throughout the presentation.

How to Use Visual Material to Support Verbal Arguments

We have already discussed the value of both representational artifacts and the words selected to support them in a presentation. Work through the exercises outlined in this book and make sure to apply a hierarchical strategy for both the imagery and the text within your presentation. Even when present for the review, text in the presentation is still very important; it can act as reinforcement to the visual argument as well as serve as a visual cue and reminder for the presenter. Arrange the argument within the presentation to support the words that you will need to be saying. Use key words that will trigger your memory in the titles, captions and labels. These are the best locations for textual reminders because they are in locations that are not embedded in a paragraph of text. It can be very difficult to find cues in a paragraph of text during a presentation; it can be downright impossible!

Group similar drawings and diagrams together so that if you get stuck in your verbal delivery you can literally look at the presentation and just follow along with the diagrams. Use this strategy as a backup method to get you back on track and continue with the presentation.

Practice and Time Your Presentation

It goes without saying that it is vital to your success to have practiced and timed the presentation long before you actually give the presentation. It is surprising, however, how many designers omit this critical step and just try to wing it. It is not enough to just read over your notes beforehand and to not practice out loud; this still counts as winging it. You may not have enough time to fully say everything you want. Understanding your time constraints and understanding actually how long it takes to say things will likely change the nature of what is said. Accelerating the rate you talk is not a solution to a time constraint. The delivery should actually be slow and relaxed, clear and concise. Practicing will make sure you can say the important ideas in the allotted time. Start with the overarching ideas and work down to specifics from there.

Effective Use of Presentation Notes

It is acceptable to use notes during your presentation. In fact, it is a really good idea. The notes should be an outline of the main points you need to cover because the ultimate goal is to be able to talk through your ideas with the jury in a discussion-style manner. A shiny, polished presentation should not be your goal for a design presentation. Design by nature is an open-ended continual discourse and the jury situation is no different. The review process should be considered as a continuation of the conversation of your design process and your work seen as the catalyst to prompt the conversation.

Since the primary endeavor of a design presentation is to direct the jury toward the conversation you want to have about the work, make sure your notes have key words and phrases that you have carefully selected to support your design argument. It happens to everyone at some point—you are standing in front of the jury and it is as if you have never seen the work that is before you. No words flow and panic sets in. This is the moment that presentation notes will save the situation. Make sure they are printed large enough that you can see them when glancing down quickly. Do not use complete sentences for the bulk of the notes. It is very difficult to find your place in a paragraph of text when panic sets in. In fact, the only time that it makes sense to write out full sentences in your presentation notes is if there is a very specific, well-crafted thesis statement—or something of that nature—that you want to read to make sure you get absolutely correct. If this is the case, state to the jury that you are going to read from your notes to make sure you get your statement exactly right and then go back to a discussion-style presentation.

Do not rely on your notes so much that you plan to read your entire presentation. It is very difficult for a jury to follow a complex design argument when it is being read. The tone of the voice tends toward monotone and makes it incredibly difficult to pick up on important points. Instead, just work from an outlined set of notes so that you can play the role of enthusiastic designer who is simply describing all of the interesting things they have been studying. This simple presentation strategy will go a long way in helping you convey your design ideas to the jury.

What to do With Your Hands

Standing before a jury is intimidating. You are completely exposed; both physically and through the exposure of your design work. It is natural to want to use your hands in some way to help mitigate this exposure. It is best to have something in your hands to help. If you have nothing in your hands, the shaking that is betraying your nerves will be more obvious. Once you notice how obvious the hand tremors are, the more they shake. It's a nasty little cycle of nervousness! It helps to acknowledge that it is normal to be nervous and that hands shaking is a normal symptom. Know that nervousness is an indication that the presenter cares about the work they've done and they care that the presentation goes well and that the work is well-received. This is not a fault in character! It is a good thing. No jury will blame you for being nervous. Just the opposite is true; a cavalier presentation is never very well received.

Having notes in your hands helps or even carrying a sketchbook that you can take notes in helps. Remember that you are attempting to start a conversation or dialog around the ideas you have been studying through the design work so taking notes may be necessary to hold ideas in your head so you can respond intelligently even while nervous.

Another good use of your hands during a presentation is to use them to point to material on the boards to support the verbal argument that is being made. It sounds simple but this is actually a relatively challenging thing to do. When pointing to material on the boards, be absolutely specific with where you are placing your hand. Make specific points with specific references on the boards. A loose, casual gesture to the visual artifact will miss your point. Place your finger exactly where intended on the board. Practice this, it is harder to do than you think!

Beware of a Defensive Stance

Be very careful during a presentation to not act in any sort of defensive manner. This doesn't mean you can't defend your design decisions and their relative outcomes but it does mean that you can't appear defensive. Presenting a project from a defensive stance creates an atmosphere of close-mindedness that is not conducive to a conversation about the work. It is important to acknowledge different points of view from the jury and try to consider them in relationship to the work you've done. It is part of the discussion of the jury that you are trying to establish. A jury that produces questions and a curiosity around the ideas is a successful jury! There will be times when you completely and utterly do not agree with what the jury is saying. Those are the times when you will need to work to simply understand what they are saying. There will also be times when the jury runs amok and simply talks about whatever they feel like talking about. There's no way to control this completely. The best you can do is outline throughout your presentation the types of ideas you would like to talk about. This is the only part within your control; use it!

Testing In-Person Presentations

Testing your presentation is slightly different than practicing it. When you test your presentation, you are testing whether or not your verbal and visual materials match and if the delivery of your argument is clear. Grab some colleagues and ask them to listen to your entire presentation. This can be done at any point along the way in the design process—the earlier and more frequently the better. Ask them to tell you what didn't make sense, which drawings seem like they are the clearest to your design argument and which ones are not. Let them tell you where they see things falling apart. Take it all in and reflect. There may be ideas you choose to ignore, that's fine. Test your presentation on as many different people as you can. This process will reveal patterns of areas that are consistently strong and consistently weak. It is better to know all of this long before the final presentation while there is still time to adjust.

Competitions and Blind Review Presentations

Competitions and blind review presentations pose additional challenges since the designer is not present to guide the reviewers verbally or by literally pointing to what they want the reviewers to understand most about their project. It is incredibly important for a project that will go through a blind review process to be very clearly organized in a visually hierarchical way such that the reviewer can make a quick pass and understand the primary points. Keep in mind the principles of the three levels of visual reading of a presentation—the high-level browse, the mid-level browse and the in-depth review—and make sure the presentation hits the design argument highlights at all three levels.

Importance of a Cohesive Textual and Visual Argument

A cohesive textual and visual argument where the words used support the visual representations and vice versa is always important in a design presentation but is even more so in a blind review. For a project presentation to be a blind review it is likely part of a competition or something of that nature and it becomes increasingly important to make sure the design argument stands out against all of the other projects being reviewed. Proper hierarchical relationships between the visual material is a must to ensure the review focus is attached to the representations that best demonstrate the spirit of the project. Proper hierarchical relationships between text as it is associated with image is also of utmost importance. Text should be used to direct the reviewer to the ideas behind the visual material. It is never enough to label a drawing just as that drawing type. For instance, do not caption a perspective view, "perspective view." Use words that are much more descriptive and demonstrate to the reviewer how they should view the image. "Looking north toward the integrated rail and subway platform zones" is much more conducive for project understanding. Instead of saying what a representation is, use the caption to tell the reviewer why it is important for it to be included in the presentation. Also, carefully consider the project title and make sure not to title the project something that is also included in the project statistics or the descriptive body text. As an example, the title "Housing in Rotterdam" simply repeats information listed elsewhere in the presentation. Instead title the project around a primary design idea so the jury can begin to think of the entire presentation through that lens.

Accept That You Are Not in Control

The truth about a blind presentation review is that the designer is ultimately not in control of what the reviewers see or understand through the visual and textual argument. The best the designer can do is to acknowledge the challenges associated with this type of review, maintain proper systems on the layouts through visual order and visual hierarchy and make sure that all of the ideas that would be presented in an in-person review are present and visible on the boards. Do your due diligence by testing again and again with your colleagues that the proper messages are being conveyed.

Testing Blind Review Presentations

Testing blind review presentations is vital to the designer's understanding of the conveyance of the design argument. In order to get a truly effective

Presentation Design—**Strategies for Different Presentation Types**

response, the designer needs to find colleagues who aren't completely familiar with the project. Have the colleagues try to point out the most important ideas in a hierarchical order as well as the representations that support those ideas. Ask your colleagues if there is clarity to the diagrams and drawings. Listen to what they are saying. It can be very difficult to change a representation type when you have been working with it and have some conviction about why it is so important. However, with a blind review since the designer is not present, it doesn't really matter what they think. What really matters is how well things are understood when the designer doesn't explain anything verbally.

Digital Presentations

Digital presentations present their own unique set of issues and opportunities. It can be a fantastic way to get a lot of visual information in front of the reviewers and, if using a slide deck, facilitates the organization of a clear, linear argument. Challenges arise pertaining to the reviewer's ability to retain visual content as the digital presentation progresses. Since a slide deck presentation relies on building a linear argument and moves through a progression of images and textual material, it can be difficult for reviewers to make connections between material when the visual cues are gone because they were on an earlier slide.

Building an Argument

Building an argument for a digital presentation is slightly different than building an argument for a print presentation. With a printed presentation, all of the visual and textual material is available at all times during the presentation. This affords the reviewer the ability to make visual and therefore idea connections across all of the visual material. With a digital presentation using a slide deck, the argument can be constructed and revealed in a logical way that builds on ideas as it progresses. The challenge here, and frankly it is a challenge and an opportunity, is that logic must prevail when moving directly from one slide to the next. Creating a linear argument relies on a connection of idea or image when moving from one point to the next. Since it will be more difficult for the reviewers to hold all of the visual content from a digital presentation, it becomes even more important to tie material together as the presentation progresses. Think of it as if you are answering the question "how does this relate to that?" each time you move between points and slides.

It is best to speak to slides that are predominantly image based. Text-filled slides are difficult to follow because they don't provide any visual material to help with retainment of content for the reviewers. Text can be very helpful toward making a complex argument but use it in the same way discussed for printed boards—as support to the message delivered through the visual artifact. Since architects and designers typically present ideas that are representations of an as-of-yet unbuilt construct, it is important that the visual content supports the argument being made. You wouldn't stand before a jury and describe a space or object you intend to design, you would show the actual representation of the space or object. This is the primary tool of the designer. Use words to either support the message of the visual or to help trigger the memory of the designer during the presentation. It is usually a combination of both.

When structuring the argument, create an outline that you can use to track the design decisions and the points you want to make. Then work to assign or develop visual content to support those points. Do not put too much visual content on each slide. It is better to have one image or a pair, set or series of images that are trying to convey a singular point. Just as with all other types of presentations outlined in this book, digital presentations must maintain design consistency throughout the visual narrative. Treat each slide in the deck as a similar piece within an overall visual system. All of the rules related to typeface selection and hierarchy, underlying grid structures, alignment rules and groupings, visual legibility of drawings and text, active areas and margins, visual and content text goals, apply to digital presentations.

Another great opportunity when building an argument with a digital presentation is the ability to literally build a sequentially assembled diagram as the presentation progresses slide to slide. For this to work, the diagram needs to have valid and clear goals to achieve with each step in the building of the diagram. A simple example could be something like the argument surrounding design decisions made for the form of a building as it relates to the site. This could be a three-dimensional or two-dimensional diagram. Thinking about it in two dimensions is probably easiest. Imagine the first slide in the series is a drawing of the site plan in context, the next slide has the exact same site drawing with sight lines drawn in, the next slide shows a block on the site in plan that has indentations that are created from where the sight lines meet the building at the ground plane, and so on and so on. You get the idea. This type of sequentially assembled diagram is a perfect way to convey complex messages in a digital slide deck!

Digital Wayfinding Systems

Digital presentations sometimes need wayfinding systems just as buildings need them. A wayfinding system typically helps people get where they need to go. A digital wayfinding system is a graphic device that is applied within the presentation to continually orient the reviewer to their location in the discussion. Think of it as a way to tell the reviewer how each point relates to the overall argument. This digital wayfinding system could be manifested in multiple ways. There could be a graphic marker at the bottom of each slide that acts as a timeline for the main points in the discussion and it shows through movement where you are in the argument. The wayfinding system could simply be a series of words that act as a title to a category of content that was outlined at the beginning of the discussion and shifts as the discussion shifts. Lots of different wayfinding ideas could work.

Slide Transitions

There are some software programs that set up slide decks that allow the presenter to select from a variety of slide transitions. It is best to avoid them all; it can be really distracting to have all of this movement happening between slides while someone is trying to follow your argument. The only slide transition to consider is the fade. Only apply the fade transition when absolutely necessary and when it helps with the legibility of an idea. Don't use the fade slide transition just because you want a transition. The content of the presentation should be visually compelling enough on its own.

Notes on Integrating Multi-Media into the Presentation

If you are working with slide decks, there is an opportunity to integrate multi-media into the presentation. It is best to either embed video within the slide deck or create a link in the presentation to launch the video in a new window. Small animations work fine embedded but if the video content is particularly large, it is best to launch an additional window. If possible, avoid closing the slide deck entirely and searching for the file to launch. Most slide deck software—and there are quite a few options—has the ability to integrate multi-media in some way. Try to make it as streamlined as possible.

Digital Color Vibrations

Color vibration can often be more pronounced with digital media because light emanates from the screen to generate the colors. Color vibrations—moments where colors tend to blur at their boundaries—typically occur in adjacent locations of complementary colors. Color vibrations also typically occur with highly saturated colors. To those with color blindness, adjacent vibrating colors tend to disappear entirely, reducing the color field to just one tone. For legibility purposes, it is best to avoid colors that vibrate against one another.

Testing for Digital Presentations

Just as with all types of presentations, digital presentations must be tested for legibility of both the visual and verbal message. Again, gather colleagues and see if what is being said in the verbal argument makes sense against the visual material being shown and the order in which it is presented. Make note of any areas of confusion and figure out what needs to be adjusted, maybe a wayfinding system is needed, maybe additional diagrams need to be drawn, maybe the choices made for the verbal argument are throwing things off.

Also, with digital presentations, it is imperative that while designing the presentation you know how and where it will be projected. It makes a big difference in

Presentation Design—**Strategies for Different Presentation Types**

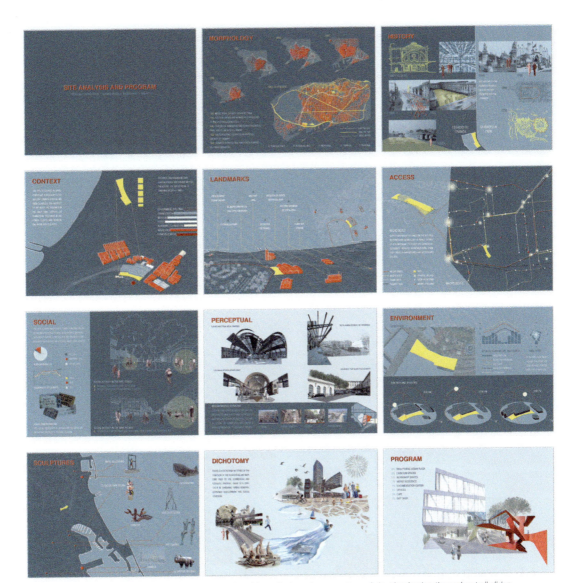

This series of presentation slides uses color and typeface hierarchy to set up a system of visual cohesion throughout all slides. Presentation by Nada Khalaf and Mariam Jacob.

how the visuals are designed if the presentation is on a large-format TV or projected on a large or even small projection screen. The quality of the projector is also an important factor to consider. If the projector available for the presentation is not high resolution, it can potentially impact the legibility of words, drawings and images. As soon as possible, figure this out and test it!

cover letters and correspondence, resumes and portfolios

presenting yourself professionally

Presenting yourself professionally is one of the more challenging tasks when transitioning from an academic community to a professional one. There are plenty of rules and guidelines to follow for appropriate communication and representation in the professional realm. This section aims to outline the basics related to developing and structuring an appropriate resume, cover letter and basic correspondence. There is also a section that defines basic principles of portfolio design along with several exemplary examples of design portfolios. For additional information on portfolio design, see: *Constructing the Persuasive Portfolio: The Only Primer You'll Ever Need* by Margaret Fletcher. Within this publication you will find detailed information on the development and construction of a design portfolio.

One of the single most important things you can do to present yourself professionally is to make absolutely certain there are no errors of any kind within your application materials. That means no spelling errors, no grammatical errors, no punctuation errors, no formatting errors and for designers who are including portfolio or presentation materials with their applications, no layout errors. This issue of no layout errors is a particular challenge since these rules can be subjective at times. This book and the previously mentioned portfolio book strive to make clear all of these graphic rules so that you can represent your best self when presenting yourself professionally.[1]

Cover Letters and Correspondence

There are several different types of correspondence that you may need to provide when applying for professional positions. The most important type is the cover letter that is sent along with your resume and perhaps some work samples—an abbreviated portfolio. There are two primary types of cover letters; one that is essentially responding to a specific advertised and available position or one that is simply a letter of interest for a firm that is not currently hiring. Both letters are very similar in nature, tone and structure.

First and foremost, your cover letter should deliver information not readily found on your resume. Instead, choose two to three traits or skills that you think will be an asset to the organization you are applying to. Define those traits or skills and give clear examples of them. If you recently graduated and don't have a lot of work experience, use this as an opportunity to describe transferable skills that you have demonstrated in an academic setting and explain how they can be helpful in a professional one. Don't highlight skills that are missing from your resume. Focus instead on the positive attributes of your experience.

Sections of a Cover Letter

A cover letter doesn't have to be overly complicated to be effective. There are four primary sections to a cover letter: the contact information, the salutation, the body of the letter, the complimentary close—such as kind regards or sincerely— with your name and signature. Within the body of the letter, there should be four paragraphs at a minimum. The first paragraph should be used to indicate why you are writing—presumably to apply for a job or express interest in a firm—and should properly introduce yourself. For an introduction, state who you are and in very clear terms what your strengths are that demonstrate your suitability for the advertised job. The second paragraph is the place where you can write with more depth about your skills and how they might apply to the position. Use specific situational examples, if possible, to support your argument. The third paragraph is reserved for you to write something about your knowledge of the company and how you can contribute to its goals and objectives. The fourth and final paragraph should provide a summary of your qualifications and should suggest next steps such as requesting an in-person or phone meeting.

How to Address the Letter

If possible, it is best to find an actual person's name to use in addressing your letter. Look this up on the company website or even call to ask. If you simply cannot find a name, use "Dear Hiring Manager" as the "to" line. If you've been introduced to the firm through an internal contact, be sure to use their name in the letter as an indication of your connection to the business.

Format

When writing a formal cover letter, use a proper business letter format. The heading of the letter should include your name and address, the name and address of the person you are writing followed by the date. Following the date comes the salutation line. Make sure to use the proper title of the person you are addressing. Then proceed with the body of the letter, a complimentary close and your name and signature.

If you are sending your cover letter within the body of an email—as you will sometimes be required to do—the format can be slightly less formal. You will also need to include an appropriate subject line. The structure of the letter should be the same. However, there is no need to include your name and address and the name and address of the person you are writing at the top of the email letter. Instead, make sure to use a proper title in your salutation and upon closing the letter, include contact information after your name.

Tone

The tone of all of your correspondence should be professional but does not need to use overly formal language. There is no need to write in a way that is unnatural. For instance, avoid formal phrasing such as "With this letter I wish to convey my heartfelt interest at the aforementioned advertised position at your esteemed organization." Also avoid common business clichés such as, "think outside the box," "go-getter," "self-starter;" you get the picture. Avoid them. Be yourself in your letter and strive to come across as the normal, polite, professional, charming person that you are.

Resume Recommendations

Believe it or not, resumes do go through visual trends and styles just as graphics do. I always advocate to avoid anything trendy and stick with the basics. That's not to say that the visual trends are wrong, just make sure that you have the basics covered before trying anything additional. As always, graphics for graphics' sake is gratuitous and can make a resume difficult to read. Since the primary objective of a resume is to deliver clear and concise information, make sure all resume visuals do not distract from this primary goal.

Format and Categories

For the purposes of this discussion only the basics for creating a resume will be discussed. As stated before, the primary goal of a resume is to provide clear and concise information about a person and their experiences as they relate to both academic and professional environments. It is best to organize a resume around a series of categories so that the information is easily digestible. The primary categories are: Contact Information, Education, Experience, Selected Honors and Awards, Activities, Special Skills and References.

The Contact Information section should have your full name, a current mailing address, a phone number and an email address. Make sure the email address is a professionally appropriate one and not the one you made up when you were twelve. You can also include a link to a professional page such as LinkedIn or to your professional web page. Typically this information is included at the top of the resume.

In the Education section, list the name of the degree and the institution where it was earned along with the years you attended. If you haven't graduated yet, you can list the expected graduation date and label it as such. It is also appropriate to include where the institution is located and your GPA. List all of the higher education institutions you have attended in reverse chronological order.

The Experience section can easily include professional experience, internship experience, academic experience or volunteer experience depending on where you are in your professional trajectory or depending upon what type of job you are applying for. In any case, list everything in reverse chronological order. For each line item under experience, include the name of the organization, its location and the dates you were there. Also include your official title and a list of responsibilities you had while you were there. For project-driven work environments such as a design firm, it is a good idea to list the projects you worked on as well.

Selected Honors and Awards can include anything that relates to this topic in really any category, so the awards could be academic, professional, personal, etc. This is a good section of the resume to capture your accolades and, as it develops over time, will start to reveal the types of things that are important to you.

The Activities section typically captures details of a more personal nature and gives you an area to fit some items onto your resume that might not fit in other places. It could list sports, arts, musical talents, things of that sort. It is also a place where you could list volunteer activities or special projects if you decided not to make a specific category for them within the experience section.

The Special Skills section will shift depending on your profession but for designers this is where you can list both digital and analog skills pertaining to representation and the profession.

And finally, always include references on your resume. It is not a good idea to list "references available upon request." This requires too much work for your resume reviewer to follow up if they are interested in you and your work. Make things easier for them, list three references on your resume. Include their titles, place of business, phone number and email. Make sure to verify inclusion with your references before adding them to your resume.

Graphic Resumes

There is growing trend in the design profession to develop graphic resumes that provide charts and infographics particularly for areas such as skills. In these instances, some sort of graphic chart describing competency is used. Be careful, after all, you are the one making the assessment of your skill level and assigning a particular rating to the skill seems very arbitrary. It is a better strategy to use words to describe digital or analog proficiencies such as; basic, intermediate or proficient.

Portfolio Design Actions[2]

Identifying the Audience

(1) *Know the requirements of your intended audience and stick to those parameters.*

(2) *Understand it is best to prepare flexible content and a flexible portfolio design to support a variety of portfolio outputs both printed and digital.*

Collect, Document and Catalog the Work

(3) *Collect all physical artifacts to be documented for possible inclusion in your portfolio. Store physical artifacts properly.*

(4) *Perform both reference documentation and presentation documentation.*

(5) *Digitally clean and edit all of the digital representations of your work.*

(6) *Store all digital material in an organized cataloging system.*

Planning the Work

(7) *Learn and understand the difference between content narrative, visual narrative and project narrative. Make purposeful decisions for each.*

(8) *Develop a flexible portfolio system.*

(9) *Design the content and design the container.*

(10) *Determine size and orientation of the portfolio.*

(11) *Identify portfolio components that need to be included.*

(12) *Develop an organizing storyboard.*

Strategies for Portfolio Organization

(13) *Organize the Content Narrative: Decide if projects will be organized in an order or by category or some combination.*

(14) *Portfolio Components: Decide which portfolio components will be used as an organizing strategy. Portfolio components to consider:*

> table of contents
> section divider spreads
> header and footers
> page numbers
> graphic icon systems

(15) *Project Components: Decide which project components will be used as an organizing strategy. Project components to consider:*

> parallel project introduction material
> consistent graphic indicators

Systems of Visual Structure

(16) *Decide on underlying structure, grid or alignment system or both.*

(17) *Design the active area.*

(18) *Design the visual relationships between objects on a page.*

(19) *Design the visual pace of the portfolio.*

Graphic Design Basics

(20) *Establish visual order and visual hierarchy.*

(21) *Get a handle on graphic rules of typography and implement them.*

(22) *Learn correct graphic punctuation and put what you've learned to good use.*

(23) *Don't screw it all up with goofy graphics.*

Project Narrative Visual Representation

(24) Determine the project narrative for each project being considered for inclusion.

(25) Decide if you have representational artifacts to match all of the ideas from the project narrative.

(26) Decide which projects should be included in your portfolio.

(27) Determine the appropriate order for each project narrative.

(28) Apply hierarchical relationships to support the project narrative.

(29) Understand best practices for typical architectural symbols and conventions and apply them.

(30) Use labeling systems appropriately.

(31) Make sure your presentation drawings are legible at the scale of the portfolio.

(32) Correct issues with image quality in your portfolio.

Text in Your Portfolio

(33) Improve your word selection throughout the portfolio.

(34) Review and implement writing tips.

(35) Understand and implement the content and visual goals of text in your portfolio.

(36) Get straight how you are approaching architecture-specific text issues in your portfolio.

Editing and Reviewing Your Work

(37) Perform a thorough visual review of your portfolio.

(38) Review your portfolio page by page against the graphics editing checklist.

(39) Review your portfolio page by page against the copy editing checklist.

The Printed Portfolio

(40) Understand different print portfolio types and determine which ones need to be produced from your designed portfolio system.

(41) Review and implement portfolio dimensions and orientation guidelines.

(42) Decide on a printing method.

(43) Decide on a binding type.

(44) Decide on cover material and design.

(45) Decide on paper type.

The Digital Portfolio

(46) Match your goals and objectives for creating a digital portfolio to the value of each digital portfolio option before embarking on a separate digital portfolio exercise.

(47) Review and implement issues related to presenting architectural work digitally.

(48) Review and implement basic web guidelines.

Visual Communication for Architects and Designers: constructing the persuasive presentation

Portfolio 01
Joana Benin

Specifications
size: 8.5" x 11", 216mm x 279mm
orientation: vertical page, horizontal spread
length: 44 pages, 7 projects in 3 sections

Strengths

portfolio organization
visual narrative

table of contents is a combination of project diagram icons and text for a clean, light graphic representation of project ideas

project diagram icons are used on project introduction spreads as a consistent graphic indicator related to the table of contents

image edges define consistent page margins and active area throughout portfolio

footer contains page numbers as primary wayfinding system

grids and margins

single page divided into two horizontal sections is a sub-organization system that appears throughout portfolio

portfolio makes good use of diagram sets and series to explain project content

image organization

generous images framed by narrow margins of left page of each project introduction spread announces the beginning of each new project

diagram series consistently provides secondary visual support to primary images

text and
typeface strategies

large, all capital letter titles on project introduction pages act as consistent graphic indicator

typeface hierarchy is established and consistent throughout portfolio

use of diagram labels and call-outs with appropriate typeface hierarchy supports visual and content goals for each

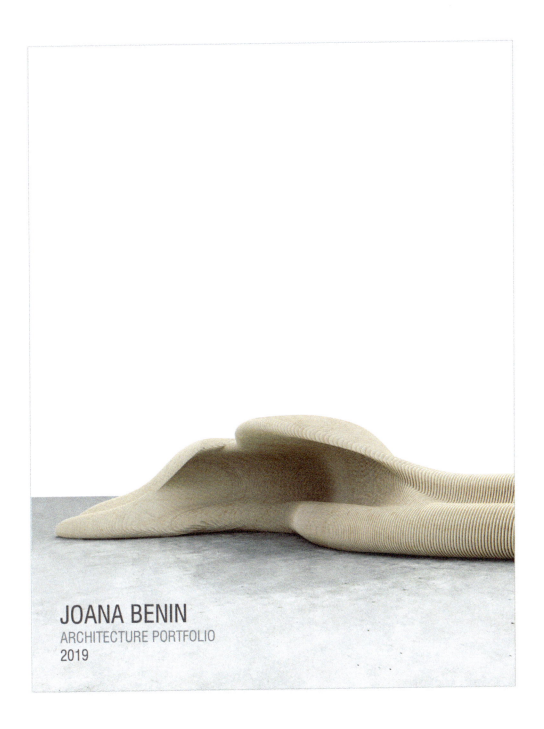

JOANA BENIN
ARCHITECTURE PORTFOLIO
2019

Visual Communication for Architects and Designers: constructing the persuasive presentation

resume

table of contents

project introduction spread

project introduction spread

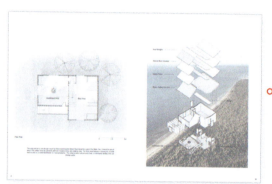

horizontal divide

horizontal divide

horizontal divide

Presenting Yourself Professionally—**Cover Letters and Correspondence, Resumes and Portfolios**

horizontal divide

horizontal divide

horizontal divide

horizontal divide

project introduction spread

project introduction spread

horizontal divide

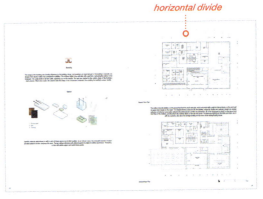

143

Visual Communication for Architects and Designers: constructing the persuasive presentation

horizontal divide

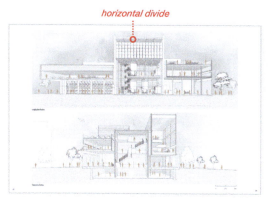

horizontal divide

horizontal divide

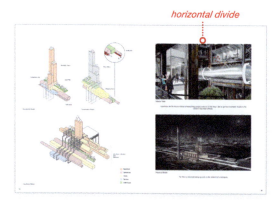

project introduction spread

project introduction spread

project introduction spread

144

Presenting Yourself Professionally—**Cover Letters and Correspondence, Resumes and Portfolios**

horizontal divide *horizontal divide* *project introduction spread*

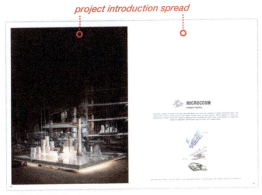

horizontal divide *horizontal divide*

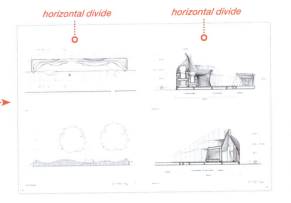
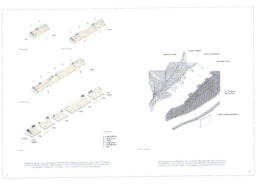

Visual Communication for Architects and Designers: constructing the persuasive presentation

Portfolio 02
Henry Savoie

Specifications
size: 8" x 8", 203mm x 203mm
orientation: square page, horizontal spread
length: 138 pages, 11 projects over 4 sections*

Strengths

portfolio organization
visual narrative

white section divider spreads clearly break sections visually

parallel project introduction graphics announce new projects—blue textured background, light circle graphic plus yellow conceptual object provide clear order for each introduction spread

dark blue photographic pages of front matter, project introduction spreads and back matter establish visual structure throughout

table of contents is text-based with an icon system to provide additional information on projects—icon categories are award, international, lighting study, rural studio and research

grids and margins

headers and footers help define a clear active area

page margins are designed effectively and maintained throughout

dynamic application of complex compound grid allows for flexible grid module groupings resulting in a great variety of image layout opportunities within a singular system

timeline arrangement and highlight color on project chronology spreads denote included projects providing a clear, concise understanding of all projects completed

image organization

use of single-edge bleeds to emphasize primary images establishes consistent image hierarchy

use of highlight color, yellow, visually anchors drawing collections

text and
typeface strategies

typeface hierarchy supports visual objectives of each layout and is prominent when needed and subordinate when images need to be predominant

highlight color, yellow, used in titles to emphasize meaning

*some pages of this portfolio were not included due to space issues

Presenting Yourself Professionally—Cover Letters and Correspondence, Resumes and Portfolios

table of contents

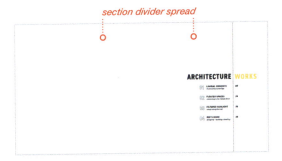

section divider spread *project introduction spread*

single-edge bleed

147

Visual Communication for Architects and Designers: constructing the persuasive presentation

single-edge bleed *project introduction spread*

portfolio break

highlight color as visual anchor

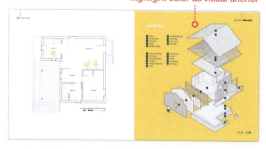

project introduction spread *single-edge bleed*

Presenting Yourself Professionally—**Cover Letters and Correspondence, Resumes and Portfolios**

single-edge bleed

single-edge bleed

section divider spread

highlight color as visual anchor

149

Visual Communication for Architects and Designers: constructing the persuasive presentation

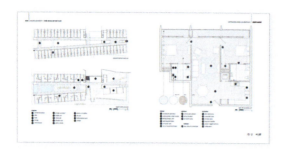

highlight color as visual anchor

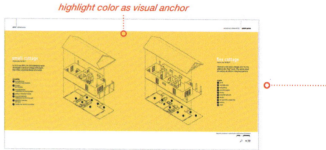

single-edge bleed   *highlight color as visual anchor*

portfolio break

Presenting Yourself Professionally—**Cover Letters and Correspondence, Resumes and Portfolios**

project introduction spread

single-edge bleed

section divider spread

project introduction spread

project introduction spread

project introduction spread

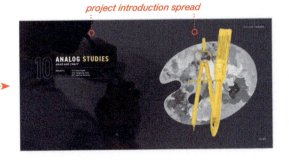

151

Visual Communication for Architects and Designers: constructing the persuasive presentation

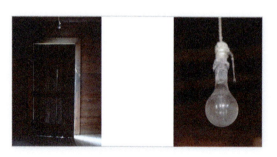

project chronology spread

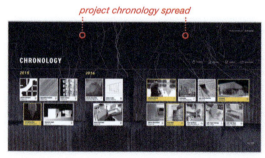

resume spread

152

Presenting Yourself Professionally—**Cover Letters and Correspondence, Resumes and Portfolios**

project introduction spread

project chronology spread   *project chronology spread*

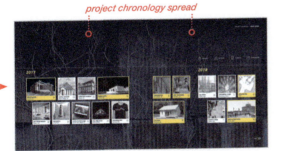

153

Visual Communication for Architects and Designers: constructing the persuasive presentation

Portfolio 03
Jianan Kang

Specifications
size: 8" x 10", 203mm x 254mm
orientation: vertical page, horizontal spread
length: 70 pages, 9 project sections*

Strengths

portfolio organization / visual narrative

table of contents is text-based and includes project title, project description and project number

right-hand page with warm tone and centrally placed justified text block marks introduction to each new project

left-hand large image extends to margins and pairs with warm-toned text page to mark introduction to each new project

grids and margins

large images push to a tight margin while lighter images, for example line drawings, float within this frame

header spans the entire spread and contains page number, project title and content type for each page

image organization

soft image colors and elegant line weights throughout the portfolio are punctuated with strong highlight color when needed

highly detailed and explanatory narrative drawings are used throughout

effective use of margins around multiple images enables them to be read as sub-sets within the layout

project content pages apply principles of image hierarchy with clear indication of primary images, secondary images and tertiary images

text and typeface strategies

consistent typeface hierarchy and placement acts as consistent graphic indicator on project introduction spreads

captions, diagram titles and labels are used to direct the reviewer to specific important visual content

*some pages of this portfolio were not included due to space issues

Presenting Yourself Professionally—**Cover Letters and Correspondence, Resumes and Portfolios**

project introduction spread

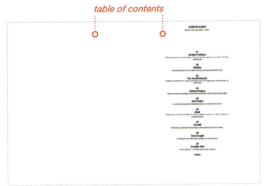

table of contents

narrative drawing *diagram sub-sets*

diagram sub-sets

narrative drawing

155

Visual Communication for Architects and Designers: constructing the persuasive presentation

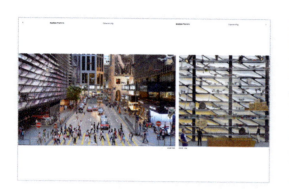

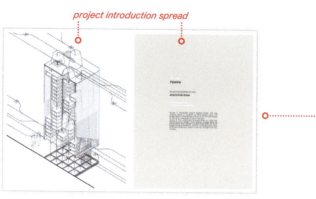

project introduction spread

diagram sub-sets

diagram sub-sets

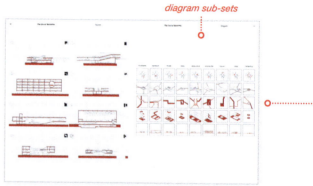

diagram sub-sets

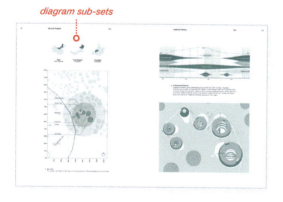

narrative drawing

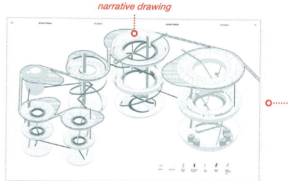

156

Presenting Yourself Professionally—**Cover Letters and Correspondence, Resumes and Portfolios**

narrative drawings

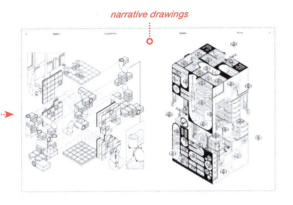

project introduction spread

project introduction spread

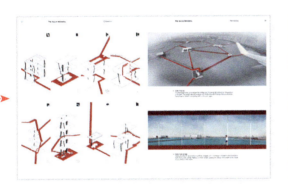

project introduction spread

diagram sub-sets

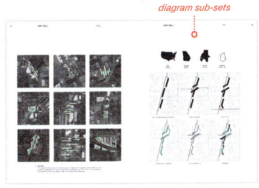

157

Visual Communication for Architects and Designers: constructing the persuasive presentation

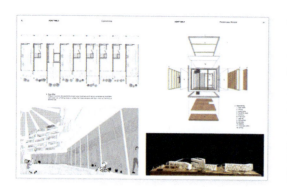

project introduction spread

diagram sub-sets

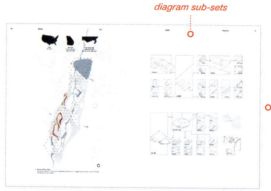

diagram sub-sets

diagram sub-sets

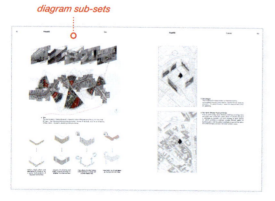

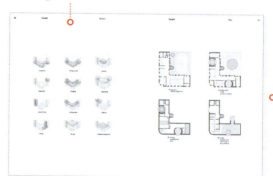

Presenting Yourself Professionally—**Cover Letters and Correspondence, Resumes and Portfolios**

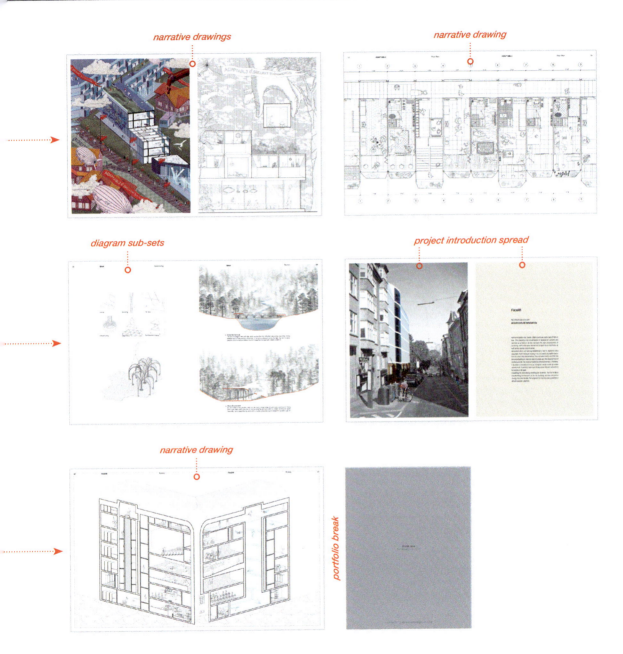

Visual Communication for Architects and Designers: constructing the persuasive presentation

Portfolio 04
William Hall

Specifications
size: 8" x 10", 203mm x 254mm
orientation: vertical page, horizontal spread
length: 96 pages, 7 project sections*

Strengths

portfolio organization
visual narrative

bold use of color announces each new project and section in the portfolio and acts as a significant element of the visual narrative

typographic table of contents provides clear wayfinding system

vertical header at left edge acts as a consistent graphic indicator on all pages and announces project title and year of completion

grids and margins

thick top and bottom margins emphasizes horizontality of the spread

primary grid is single column and is used to visually emphasize imagery while text does not adhere to that system and instead floats to offer visual balance of the purposeful offset of layout

image organization

typically no more than one image per page or spread focusing attention to the strength of those graphics

single-edge image bleeds are used to activate the layout and emphasize the graphic offset

text and
typeface strategies

uniform width of text block establishes strong consistency that allows for freedom from regular placement therefore text box can float to establish visual balance

large, graphic quality of project titles on project introduction pages act as consistent graphic indicator and are so visually strong that they can float around the page on different layouts but are still clearly understood as part of the same system

*some pages of this portfolio were not included due to space issues

160

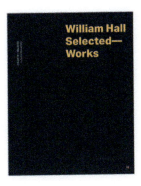

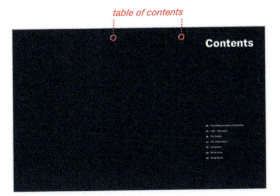
table of contents

project introduction spread

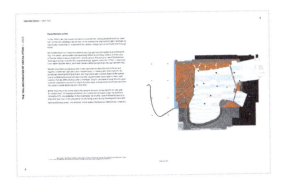

portfolio break

Visual Communication for Architects and Designers: constructing the persuasive presentation

project introduction spread

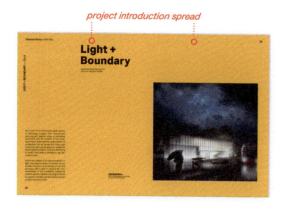

single-edge bleed

project introduction spread

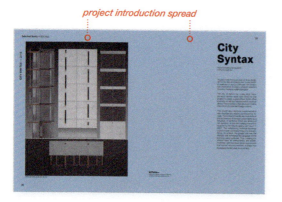

single-edge bleed

project introduction spread

single-edge bleed

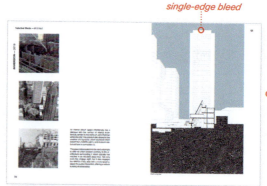

Presenting Yourself Professionally—**Cover Letters and Correspondence, Resumes and Portfolios**

single-edge bleed

single-edge bleed

portfolio break

project introduction spread

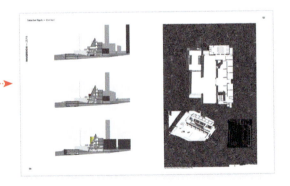
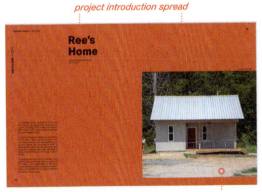

single-edge bleed

163

Visual Communication for Architects and Designers: constructing the persuasive presentation

single-edge bleed

project introduction spread

single-edge bleed

single-edge bleed

164

Presenting Yourself Professionally—**Cover Letters and Correspondence, Resumes and Portfolios**

single-edge bleed

single-edge bleed

single-edge bleed

single-edge bleed

resume spread

portfolio break

165

case study examples

drawing for impact

There are many types of drawings that are necessary for a successful presentation. Typically, basic drawing sets are defined as a requirement of a project. These guidelines should be considered a minimum of what might be needed to convey design ideas. The single most important thing you can do to strengthen your design argument is to determine for yourself which drawing types are most important to convey the issues you deem to be most significant to your project. You could focus on multi-view drawings—those drawings that require multiple views to put a three-dimensional image together; plan, section, elevation—or you could focus on single-view drawings—those drawings that can convey complex spatial ideas on their own; typically paraline (axonometric, isometric, etc.) projections or perspective projections. In developing your representations, don't forget about the power of a good diagram or diagram set. These drawing types have the ability to directly convey very specific ideas about a project and if designed successfully, are vital to the legibility of your project.

Aside from drawing types, there are lots of other things to think about when developing project representations. Developing a specific drawing or illustration style has become a more and more modern way to convey ideas through two-dimensional representation. It takes time to develop a drawing or illustration style that resonates with the ideas of a project and it is best to begin early to develop not only what a drawing conveys but also how it will look.

The atmospheric quality is also an important idea to think about. This idea is typically discussed with single-view drawings such as perspective projections or paraline projections. The atmosphere of a drawing has a lot to do with the drawing's ability to express experiential quality of a place or space. This atmosphere can be conveyed through both the development of drawing style and through the development of drawing content.

Another drawing objective to be aware of is a drawing that conveys a narrative of some kind. Drawing as narrative is a relatively broad category but be aware that a standard representation artifact can convey narrative information and not only technical or spatial information. Narrative information is folded into a drawing by including some element of the representation of time. There are plenty of ways to do this, let your imagination guide you!

This section aims to demonstrate a wide variety of drawing types, illustration styles, atmospheric drawings and narrative drawings. Use them as inspiration to think through the opportunities in your own work!

Visual Communication for Architects and Designers: constructing the persuasive presentation

above and right: Drawing selections from The Cloud House by Hannah Schafers.

Drawing for Impact—**Case Study Examples**

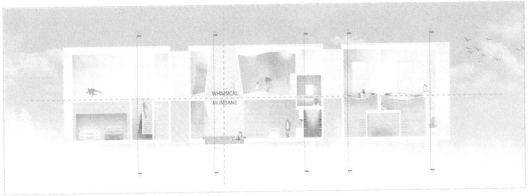

Visual Communication for Architects and Designers: constructing the persuasive presentation

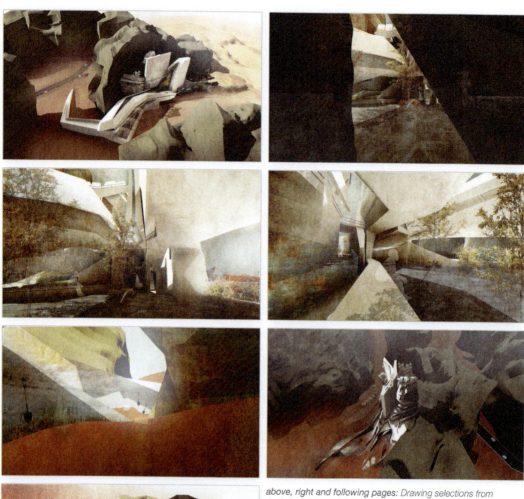

above, right and following pages: Drawing selections from *Asylum: A Place of Refuge* by Marwah Osama with Michael Hughes and Fernando Menis.

170

Drawing for Impact—**Case Study Examples**

Visual Communication for Architects and Designers: constructing the persuasive presentation

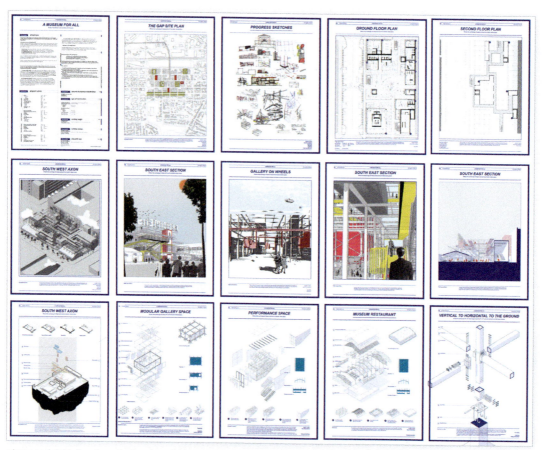

above and right: Drawing selections from A Museum for All by Berke Kalemoglu.

Drawing for Impact—**Case Study Examples**

Collective Museum   A MUSEUM FOR ALL   *Birmingham, Alabama*

WEST ENTRANCE

From across the street: Expressing the complexity of the building by turning it inside out and placing the circulation elements on the exterior aims to create a welcoming environment from the second building is visible to one. These features will grab pedestrians directly from the public sidewalks into the center of the gallery. This view highlights the legibility of the staircases, elevator units and the open ground floor entrance on the west wing.

**public realm
city and context**

legibility

Visual Communication for Architects and Designers: constructing the persuasive presentation

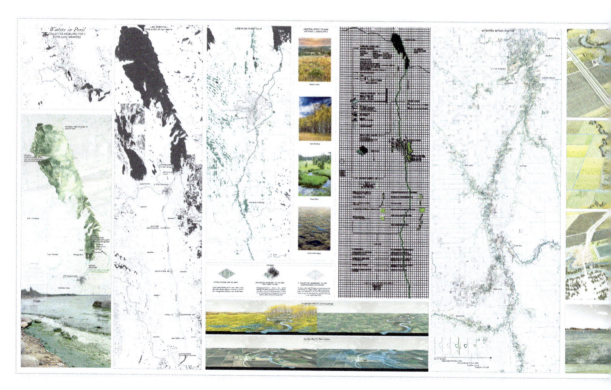

Drawing for Impact—**Case Study Examples**

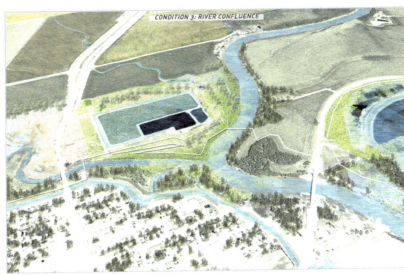

Drawing selections from Waters in Peril: Collective Measures for a Dying Lake Winnipeg by Jaysen Ariola.

Visual Communication for Architects and Designers: constructing the persuasive presentation

178

Drawing for Impact—**Case Study Examples**

above and left: Selections from Wild City by Margaret Ndungu.

Visual Communication for Architects and Designers: constructing the persuasive presentation

Drawing for Impact—**Case Study Examples**

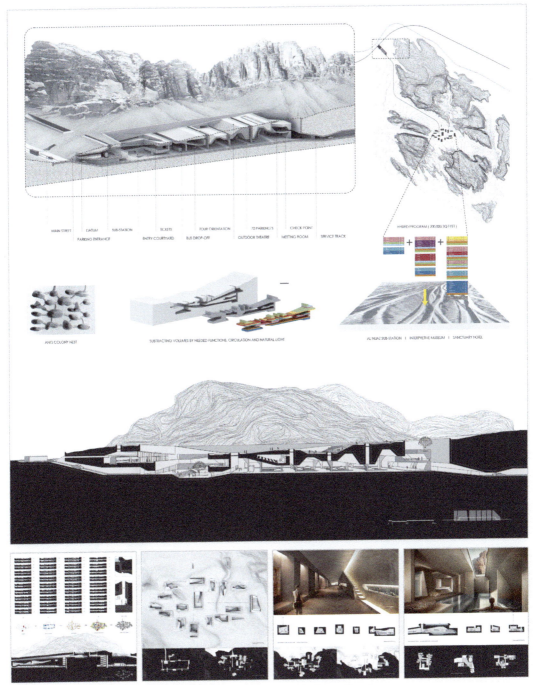

above and left: Drawing selections from Wadi Rum Excavated Sanctuaries by Rasem Kamal.

Drawing for Impact—**Case Study Examples**

above and left: Drawing selections from *London Physic Gardens: A New Necropolis* by Sam Coulton.

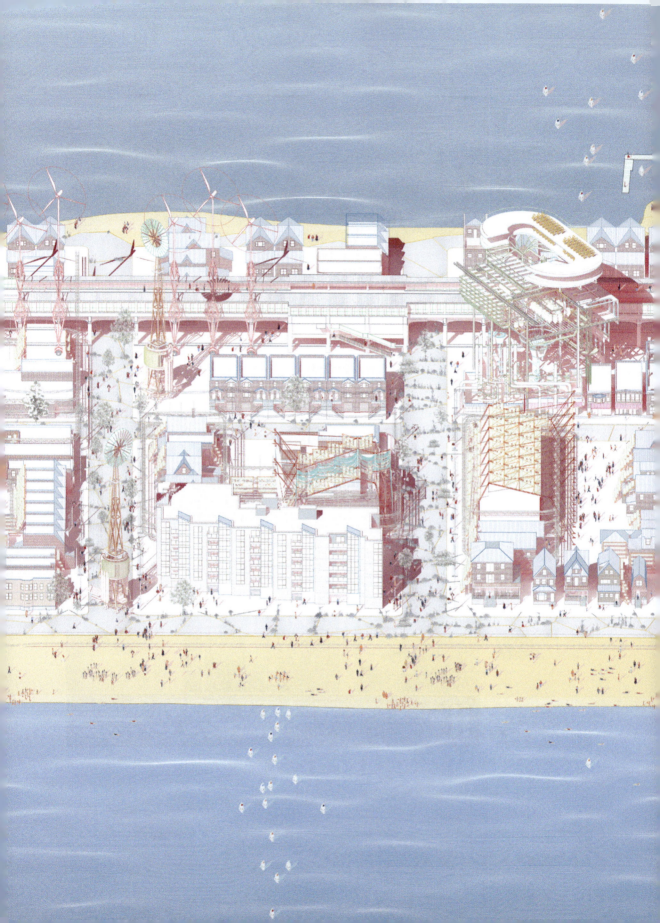

Drawing selection from The Rockaway: Climate Change and Food Crisis by Chang Cheng and Xiaodan Ma.

Visual Communication for Architects and Designers: constructing the persuasive presentation

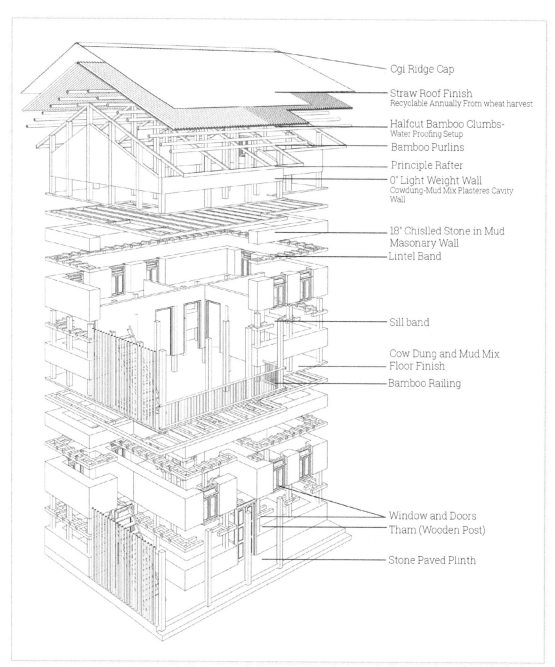

Drawing selection from Build Back Strong: Permanent Shelter Prototype in Nepal by Gaurav Neupane, Sanjeev Shrestha, Prakash Maharjan and Sajan Tamrakar.

Drawing for Impact—**Case Study Examples**

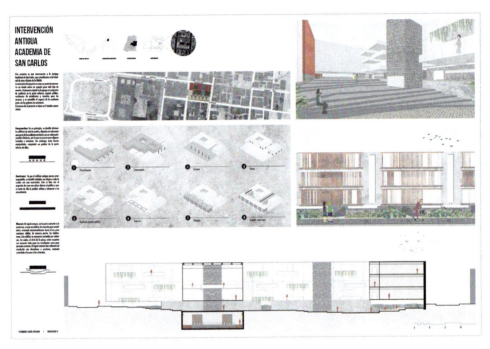

Drawing selections from Intervención Antigua Academia de San Carlos by Fernanda García Gregori.

Visual Communication for Architects and Designers: constructing the persuasive presentation

Drawing for Impact—**Case Study Examples**

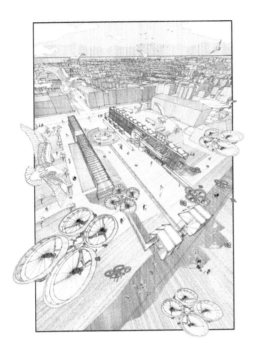
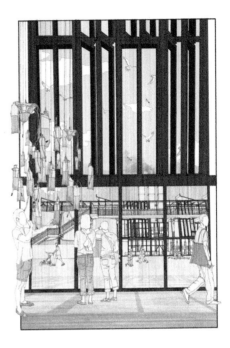
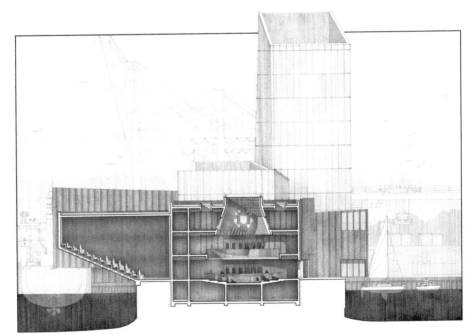

above and left: drawing selections from Hansa Peninsula: A New Home for the Hanseatic League by Fergus Littlejohn.

Visual Communication for Architects and Designers: constructing the persuasive presentation

Drawing for Impact—**Case Study Examples**

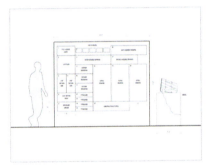

above and left: Drawing selections from *Constructed Sites // Sacred Architectonics* by Stephanie Tang.

Visual Communication for Architects and Designers: constructing the persuasive presentation

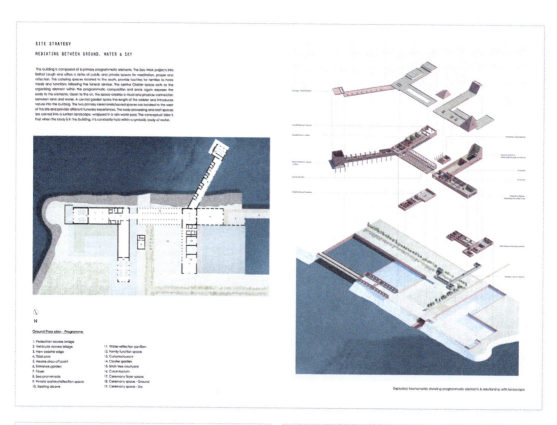

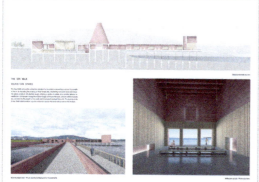

Drawing selections from Memento Mori: The Ritualized Body and The Elements by Chris McAvoy.

Drawing for Impact—**Case Study Examples**

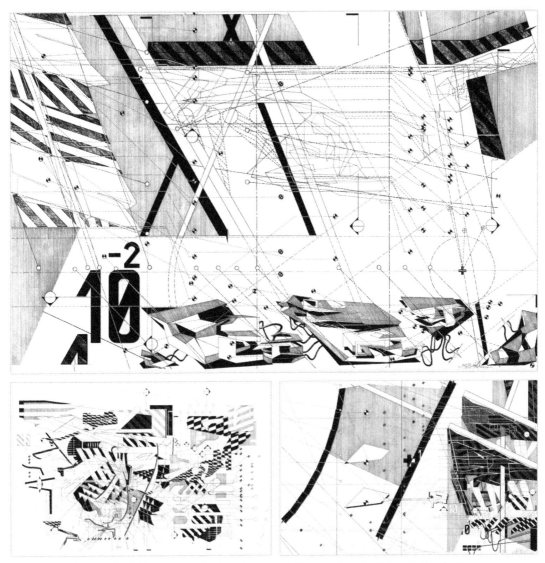

Drawings titled from top: Centiclaimer: Choose Your Lane, Microcosmic Tarmac *and* Terminal Exfoliation *by Ty Skeiky.*

Visual Communication for Architects and Designers: constructing the persuasive presentation

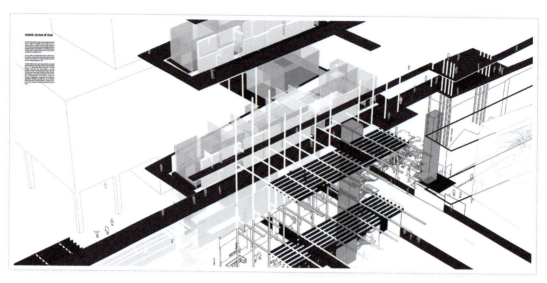

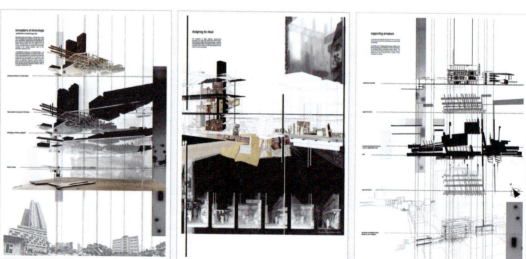

Selections from Armature of Informal Trade by Zoe Latham and Alitsia Lambrianidou.

Drawing for Impact—**Case Study Examples**

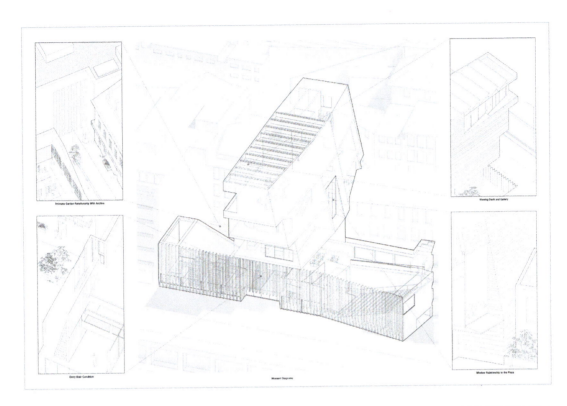

Drawing selections from Center for Portuguese Culture by Andrew Hong.

Visual Communication for Architects and Designers: constructing the persuasive presentation

Under the Skin: Moments of Paradise and Overall Strategy: Moments of Paradise by Sun Yen Yee.

Drawing for Impact—**Case Study Examples**

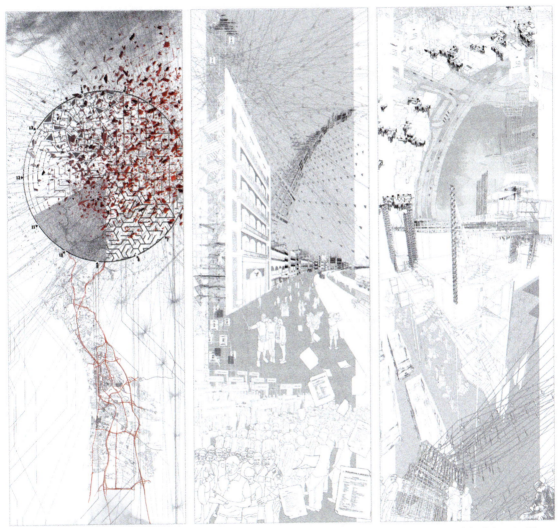

Urban Growth and The Forgotten Migrants Workers, Under the Skin: Fake Urban Front and the Truth and Under the Skin: Subversive Urban Layer for Migrant Workers by Sun Yen Yee.

Visual Communication for Architects and Designers: constructing the persuasive presentation

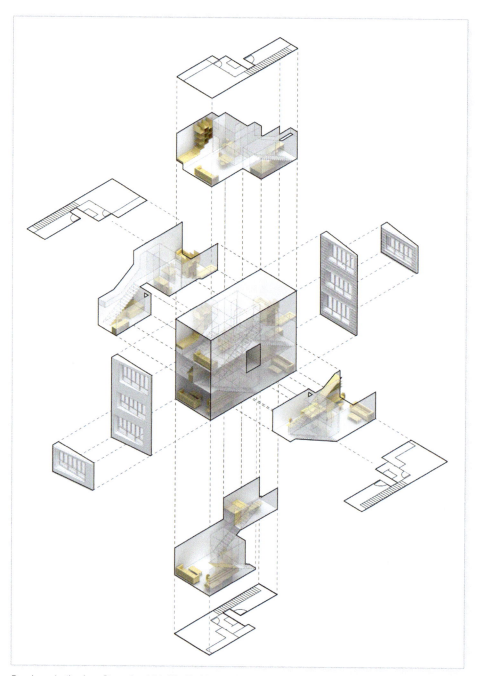

Drawing selection from Streamline: High Rise Residential, Chinatown, Oakland by Caroline Dunn.

Drawing for Impact—**Case Study Examples**

Drawing and model selections from & Other Waters, The Year-Glass of Óbuda Island by Emily Clowes.

Visual Communication for Architects and Designers: constructing the persuasive presentation

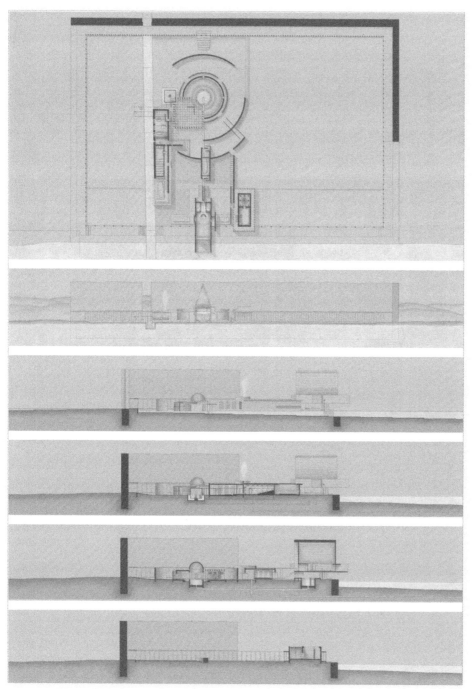

Drawing selections from Equilibrium: Between the Human Body and Nature by Barbara Ruech.

Drawing for Impact—**Case Study Examples**

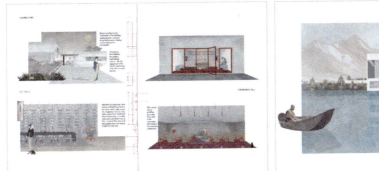

Drawing selections of a mortuary design titled Passing Light by Li Shan.

Visual Communication for Architects and Designers: constructing the persuasive presentation

above and right: Drawing selections from *Seasonal Dense(cities): Living Typologies for Future London* by Shi Yin Ling.

Drawing for Impact—**Case Study Examples**

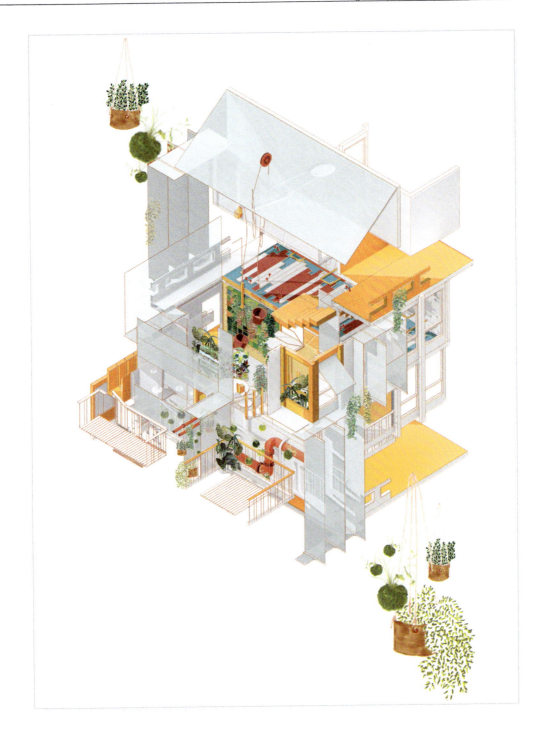

Visual Communication for Architects and Designers: constructing the persuasive presentation

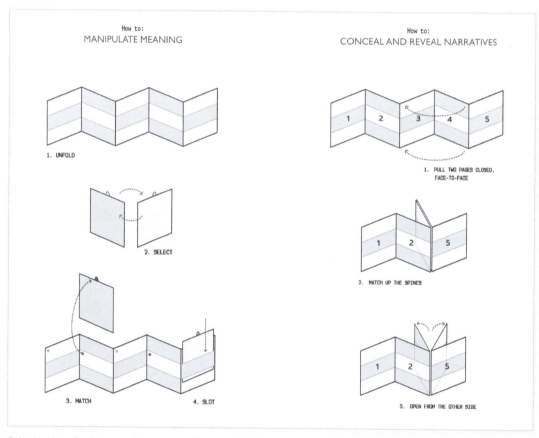

Selections from The Subverse: Monuments to Hypertextuality | The Other Side of the Story of the Other Side by Sarah Treherne.

Drawing for Impact—**Case Study Examples**

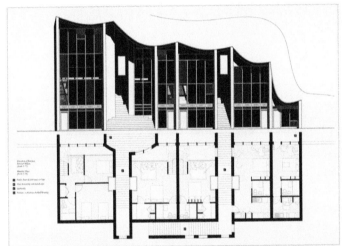

Drawing selections from Pastoral Fields by Paresh Parmar.

205

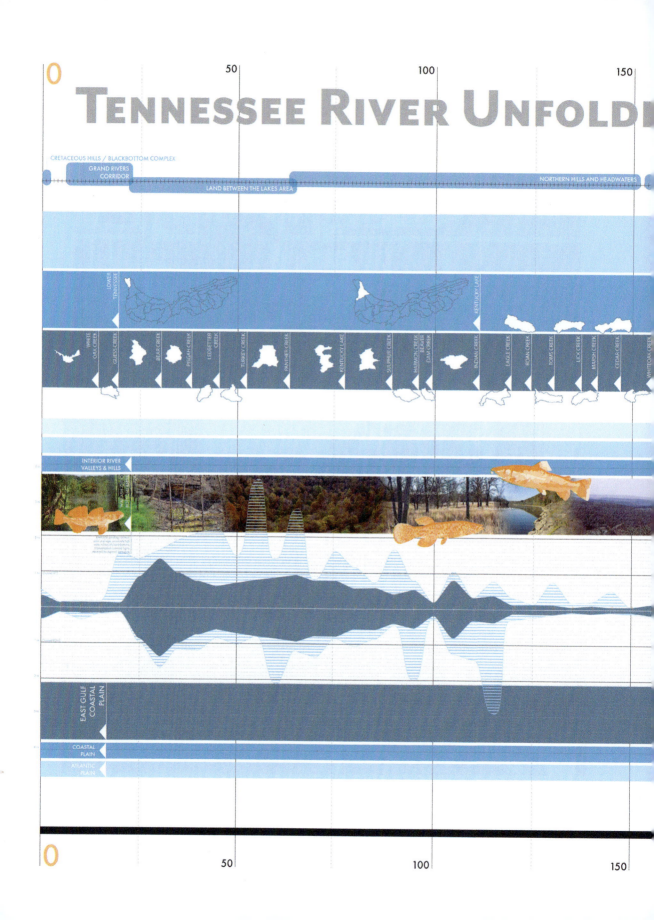

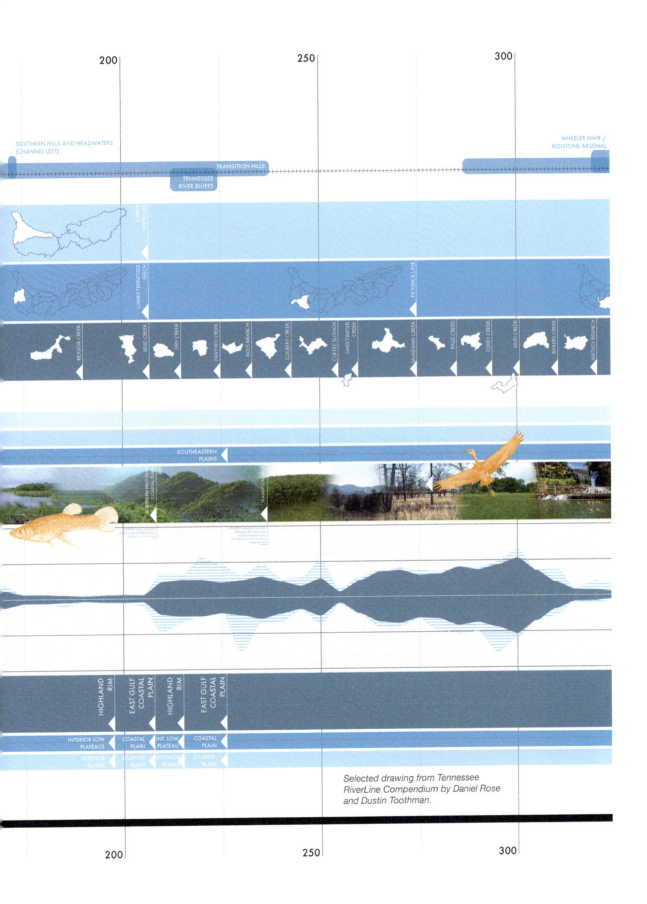

Selected drawing from Tennessee RiverLine Compendium by Daniel Rose and Dustin Toothman.

Drawing for Impact—**Case Study Examples**

above and left: Drawing selections from In Between Pitched Roof and Modernist Slab by Francisco Ramos Ordóñez.

Visual Communication for Architects and Designers: constructing the persuasive presentation

Drawing selection from Genealogy of Faulty Sequences by Meghan Quigley.

Drawing for Impact—**Case Study Examples**

Drawing selection from A Choreographed Timeline: Rewriting RIBA Building Contract by Camille Bongard.

Visual Communication for Architects and Designers: constructing the persuasive presentation

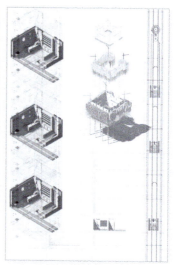

above and right: Drawing selections from {Re}casting Excursion: The Beguiled City, A Critique on Venice's Tourism Industry by Caitlin Owens.

Drawing for Impact—**Case Study Examples**

Visual Communication for Architects and Designers: constructing the persuasive presentation

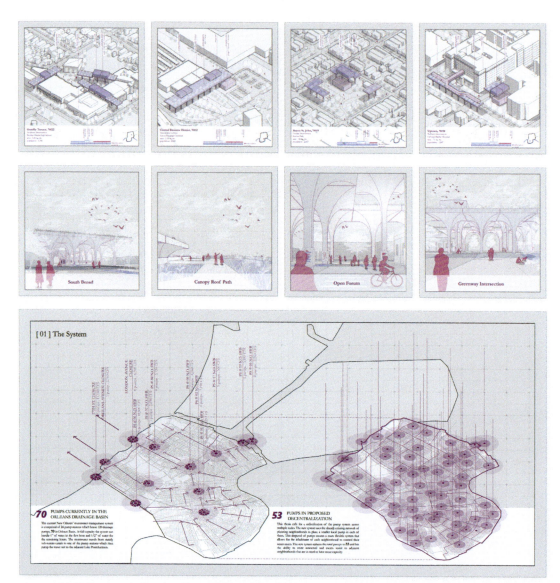

above and right: Drawing selections from *Pumps Politikos: A Novel Archetype Promoting an Alternative Urban Metabolism* by Riley Lacalli.

Drawing for Impact—**Case Study Examples**

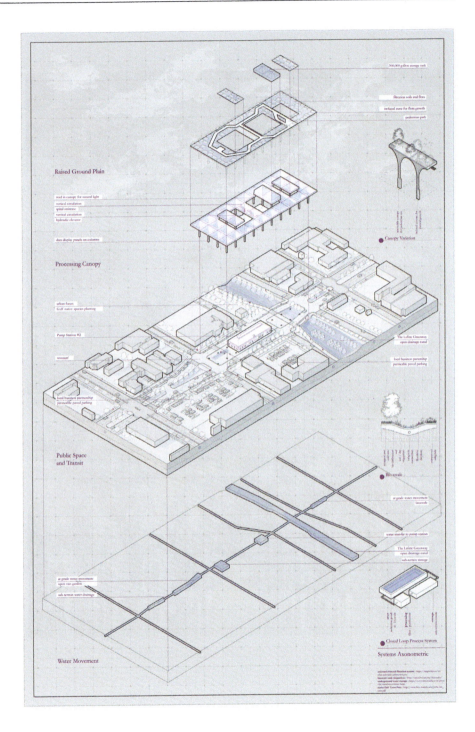

215

Visual Communication for Architects and Designers: constructing the persuasive presentation

The Time Cycle from Above the Clouds | Colonization in a Post-Nuclear War Scenario by Stanley Ka Chun Leung.

Drawing for Impact—**Case Study Examples**

Fig 5. The Recurrence

As time marches on and memories fade, so did the differences and tensions between the one percent and the population. Only recalled as an old man's tale, the catastrophic events that preceded our current situation no longer contain those who wish to challenge those in power demanding a different social and political structure. A change to a stagnant society often happen in a blink of an eye.

The Recurrence from Above the Clouds | Colonization in a Post-Nuclear War Scenario by Stanley Ka Chun Leung.

Visual Communication for Architects and Designers: constructing the persuasive presentation

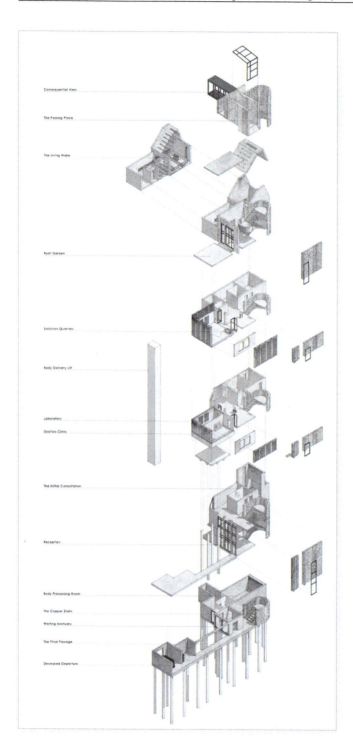

Drawing for Impact—**Case Study Examples**

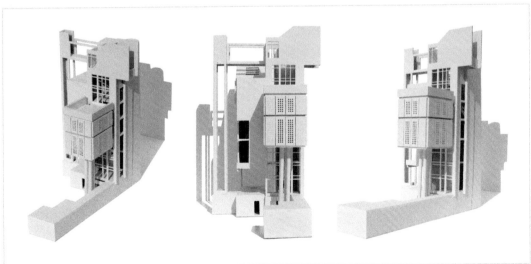

above and left: Drawing selections from The End. Designing Death by Billy Taylor.

Visual Communication for Architects and Designers: constructing the persuasive presentation

above and right: Drawing selections from Razzmatazz by Adriana F. Davis.

Drawing for Impact—**Case Study Examples**

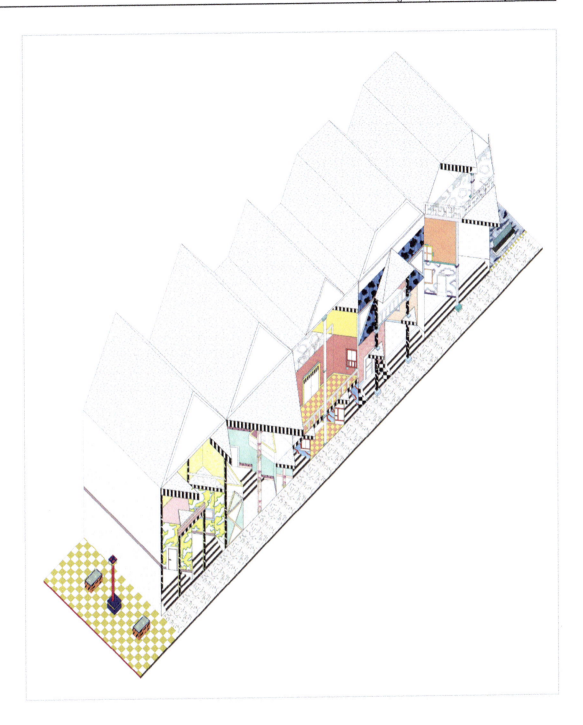

Visual Communication for Architects and Designers: constructing the persuasive presentation

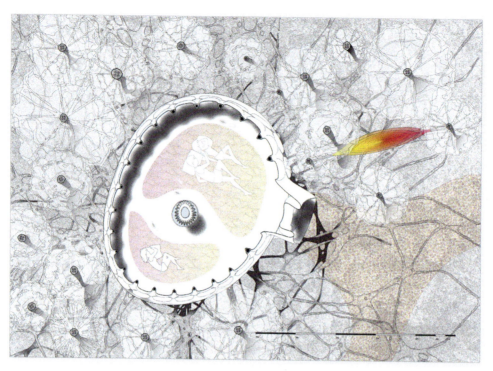

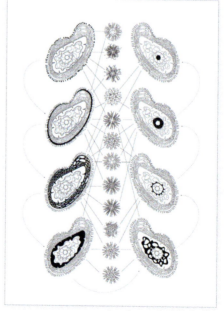

above and right: Drawing selections from E-topia: In Search of Next Nature Architecture by Alexandra Lacatusu with Toby Shew, Owen Hughes Pearce and Maria Faraone.

Drawing for Impact—**Case Study Examples**

Visual Communication for Architects and Designers: constructing the persuasive presentation

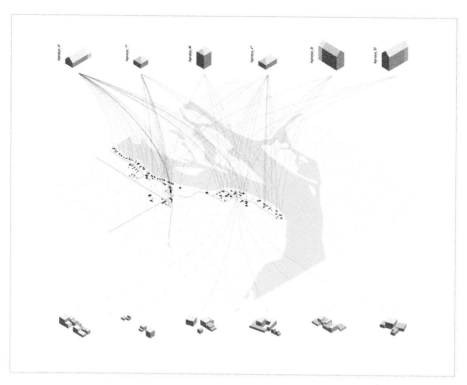

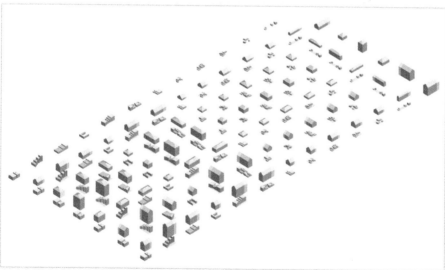

Drawing selections from Interpreting the Landscape by Trey McMillon.

Drawing for Impact—**Case Study Examples**

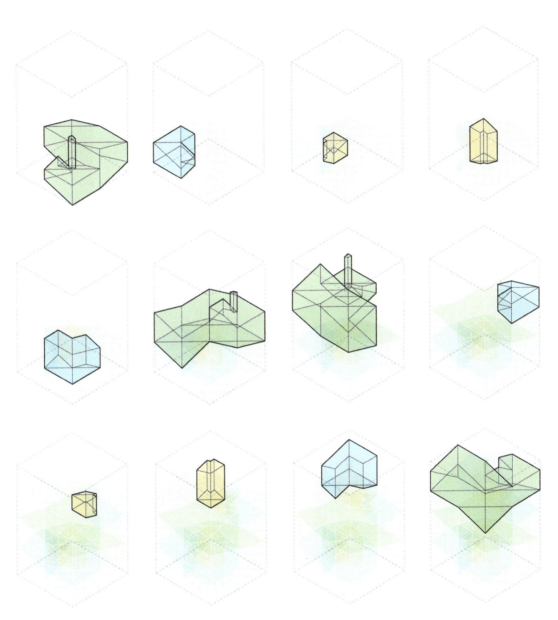

Drawing selections from Puzzle: Quilting from Rotation and Reflection by Katie Koskey.

Visual Communication for Architects and Designers: constructing the persuasive presentation

226

Drawing for Impact—**Case Study Examples**

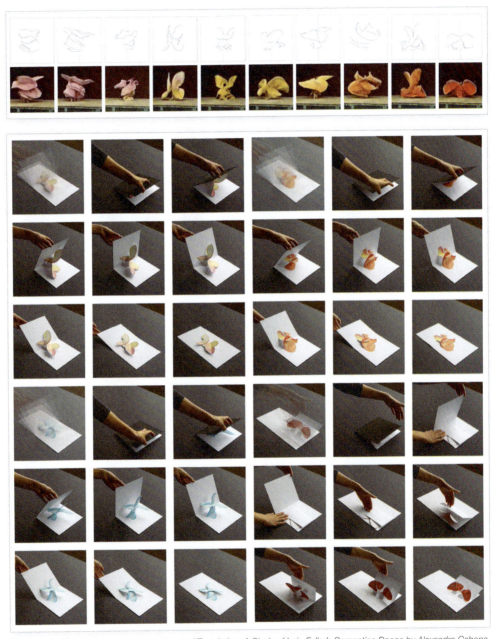

above and left: Selections from Mechanisms of Translation: A Study of Loie Fuller's Serpentine Dance by Alexandra Cabana.

Visual Communication for Architects and Designers: constructing the persuasive presentation

Drawing for Impact—**Case Study Examples**

above and left: Drawing selections from Białystok University Library by Anna Jankowska.

Visual Communication for Architects and Designers: constructing the persuasive presentation

Drawing selections from Wework Tower by Chang Liu and Jingxiao Zhou.

Drawing for Impact—**Case Study Examples**

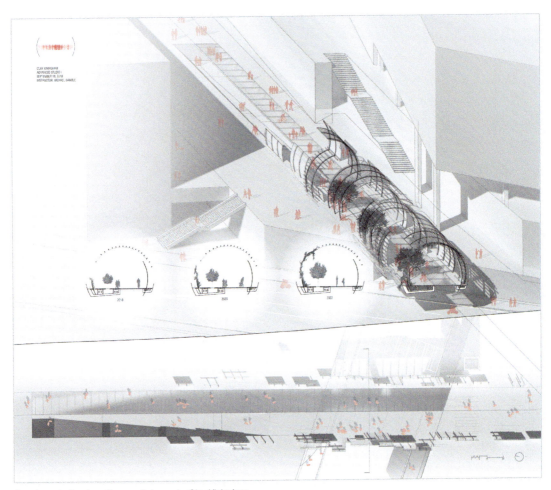

Drawing selection from Happen Between by Clay Kiningham.

Visual Communication for Architects and Designers: constructing the persuasive presentation

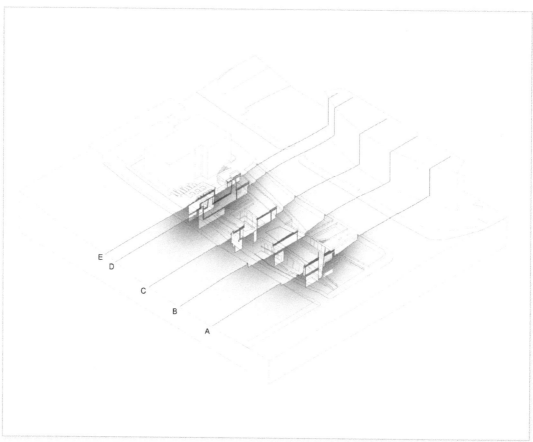

Drawing selection from Responding to Richter by Danny Griffin and Katie Koskey.

Drawing for Impact—**Case Study Examples**

Drawing selection from Storageland by Jing Liao.

233

Visual Communication for Architects and Designers: constructing the persuasive presentation

Drawing for Impact—**Case Study Examples**

above, left and following pages: Drawing selections from 2100 Macau, China: Shifting Attitudes for our Vulnerable Future by Samantha Hamilton, Eva Pontika and Charlie Glenton.

above, right and previous pages: Drawing selections from *2100 Macau, China: Shifting Attitudes for our Vulnerable Future* by Samantha Hamilton, Eva Pontika and Charlie Glenton.

Drawing for Impact—**Case Study Examples**

Visual Communication for Architects and Designers: constructing the persuasive presentation

238

Drawing for Impact—**Case Study Examples**

above and left: Drawing selections from *Materializing Sand: The Dunes, The Archipelago, The Beach* by Lin Derong. Above, progression drawings and left, situational drawings.

239

Visual Communication for Architects and Designers: constructing the persuasive presentation

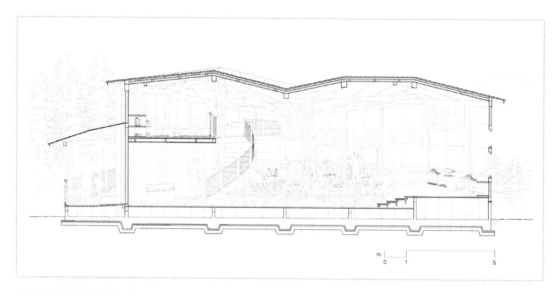

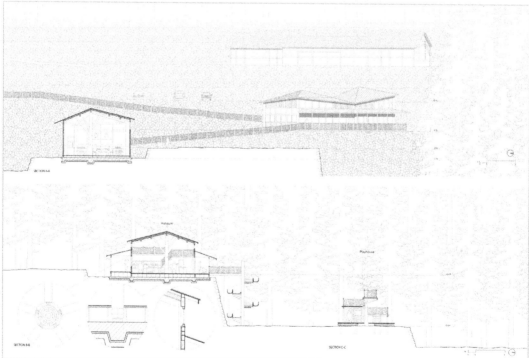

Drawing selections from Make, Play, Display by Cherry Yang.

Drawing for Impact—**Case Study Examples**

Drawing selection from Waking (Uncanny) Dreaming by Eilis Finnegan.

Visual Communication for Architects and Designers: constructing the persuasive presentation

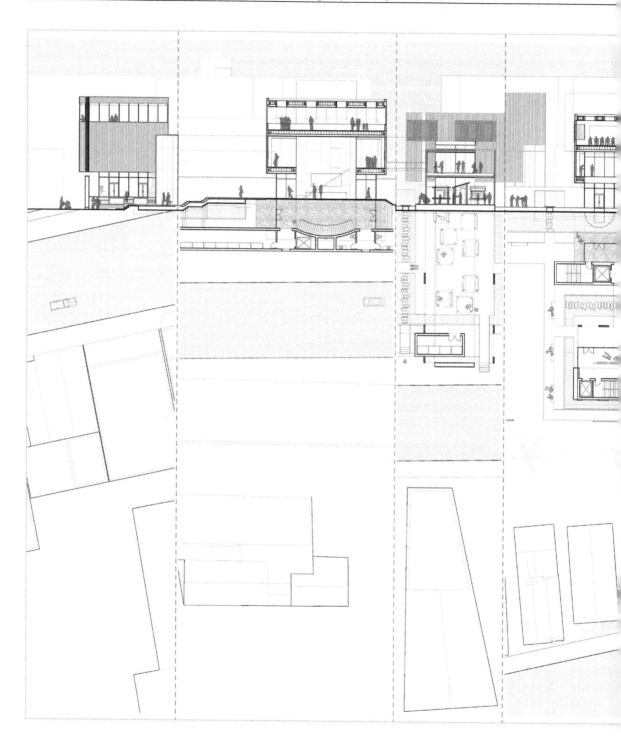

Drawing for Impact—Case Study Examples

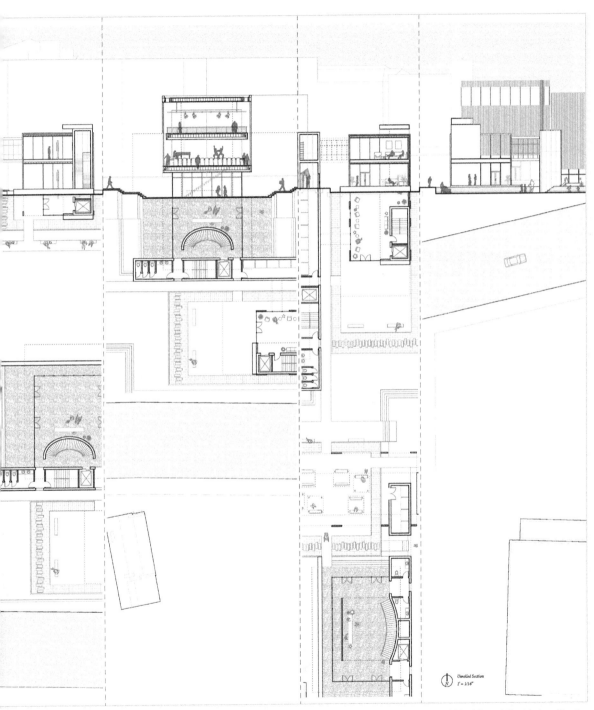

Drawing selection from A Living Memorial by Meghan Royster.

Visual Communication for Architects and Designers: constructing the persuasive presentation

Drawing selection from *Poole's Agora: A New Conviviality and Gastronomic Townscape* by Annalaura Fornasier.

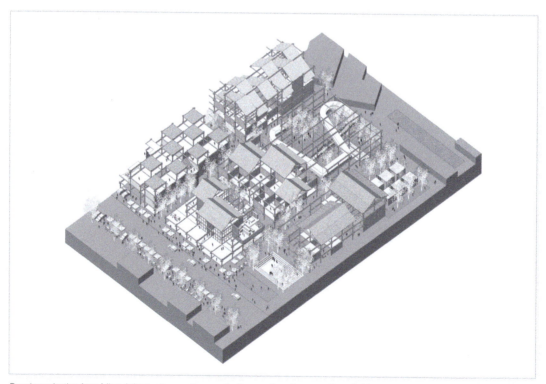

Drawing selection from *Micro-Infrastructure as Community Preservation: Kampung Baru* by William Baumgardner, Chenyuan Gu and Dandi Zhang.

Drawing for Impact—**Case Study Examples**

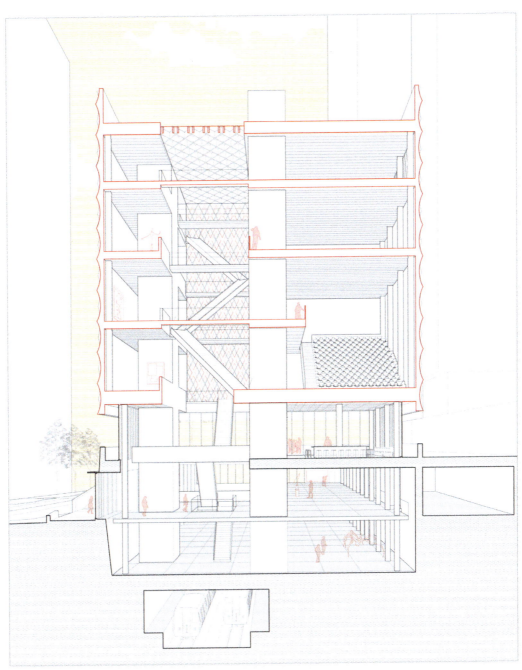

Drawing selection from A New Home for the Atlanta Contemporary Art Center by Kyle Anderson.

Visual Communication for Architects and Designers: constructing the persuasive presentation

Drawing for Impact—**Case Study Examples**

above and left: Drawing selections from Coney Island YMCA by Zhicheng Xu.

Visual Communication for Architects and Designers: constructing the persuasive presentation

Drawing for Impact—**Case Study Examples**

above and left: Drawing selections from Project Replay by Michelle Badr and Katharine Blackman.

Visual Communication for Architects and Designers: constructing the persuasive presentation

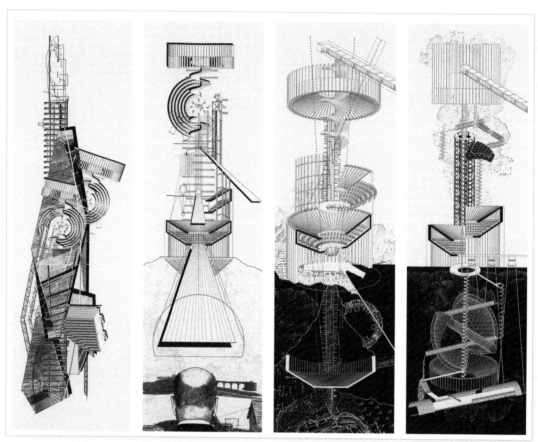

Drawing selections from Ballard's Tachistoscope by Daniel Elkington.

Drawing for Impact—**Case Study Examples**

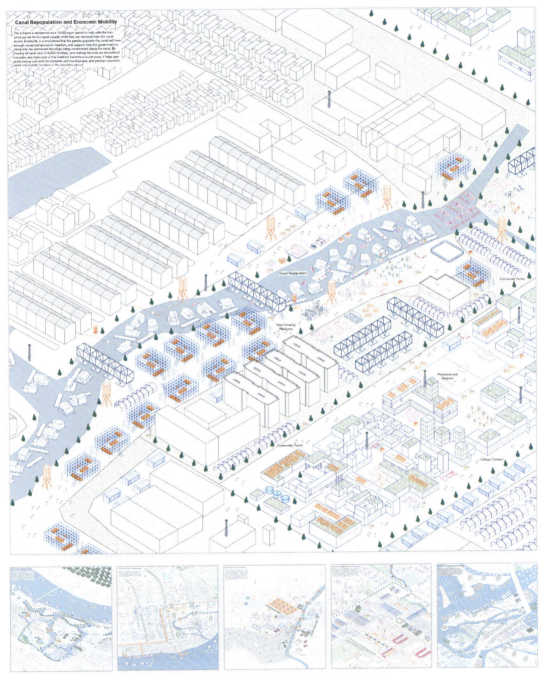

Drawing selections from Post Zone Scenarios for Ho Chi Minh City, Vietnam by Chau Tran.

Visual Communication for Architects and Designers: constructing the persuasive presentation

Drawing for Impact—**Case Study Examples**

above, left and following pages: Drawing selections from *The Ministry of Ocean Wisdom* by Victor Moldoveanu.

Visual Communication for Architects and Designers: constructing the persuasive presentation

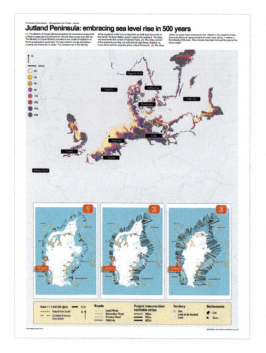
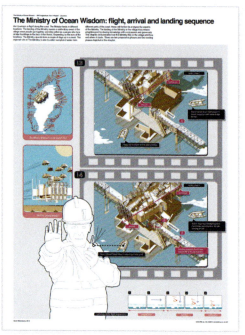
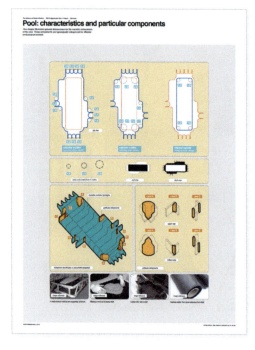
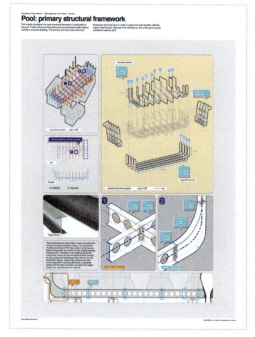

Drawing for Impact—**Case Study Examples**

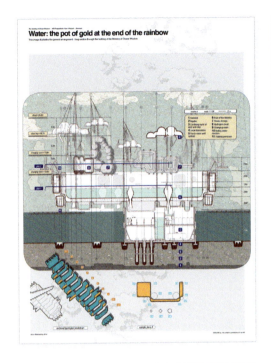

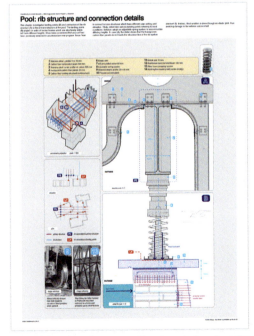
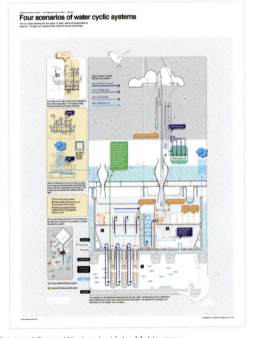

above, left and previous pages: Drawing selections from The Ministry of Ocean Wisdom *by Victor Moldoveanu.*

255

Visual Communication for Architects and Designers: constructing the persuasive presentation

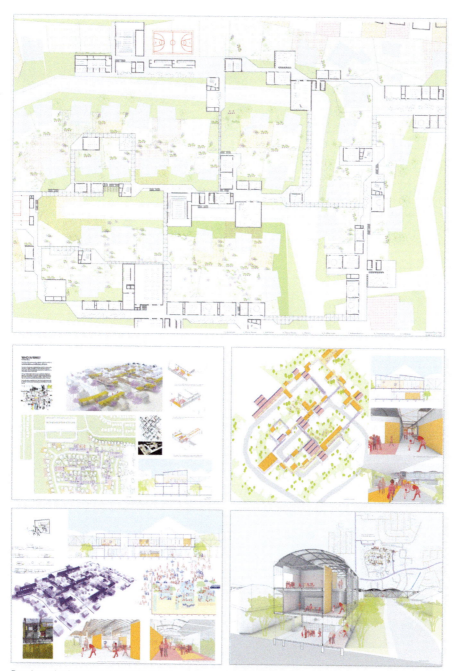

Drawing selections from Who is Who? Between Fences by Petra Salameh.

Drawing for Impact—**Case Study Examples**

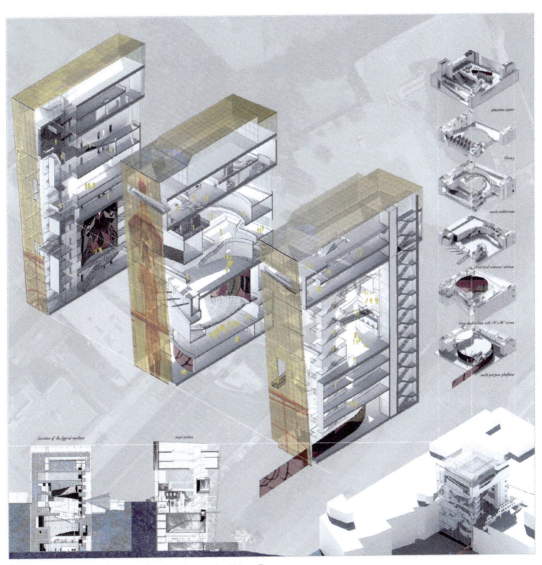

Drawing selections from Rochester Imaging Museum by Helena Rong.

Visual Communication for Architects and Designers: constructing the persuasive presentation

this page and right: Drawing and model selections from Muwaileh Public Library by Mariama M.M. Kah.

Drawing for Impact—**Case Study Examples**

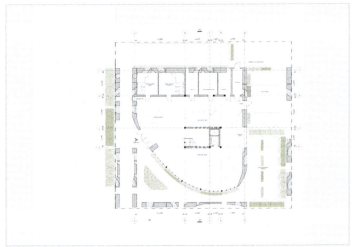

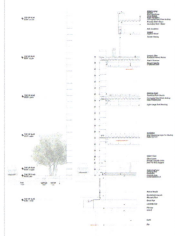

259

Visual Communication for Architects and Designers: constructing the persuasive presentation

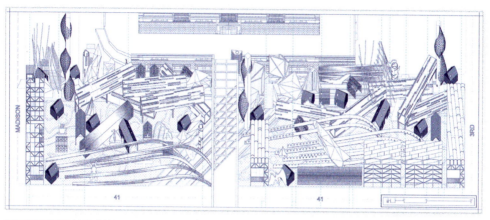

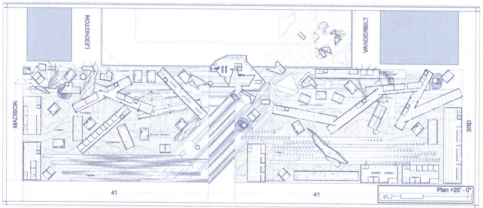

Drawing selections from MI(E)SSING WALL by Gary Chung.

Drawing for Impact—**Case Study Examples**

Drawing selections from Building up in Flames: Drawing the Counter-Memorials of the Arson Attack by Hallie Black.

Visual Communication for Architects and Designers: constructing the persuasive presentation

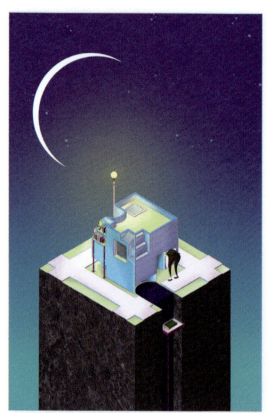

above and right: Drawing selections from Rowntree's Library for Precious Books by Stephanie Elward.

Drawing for Impact—**Case Study Examples**

 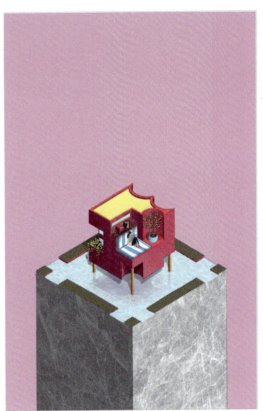

Visual Communication for Architects and Designers: constructing the persuasive presentation

above and right: Drawing selections from *Through the Plan of St. Gall: Monastic Rituals in Architecture and Landscape* by Meghan Royster.

Drawing for Impact—**Case Study Examples**

Visual Communication for Architects and Designers: constructing the persuasive presentation

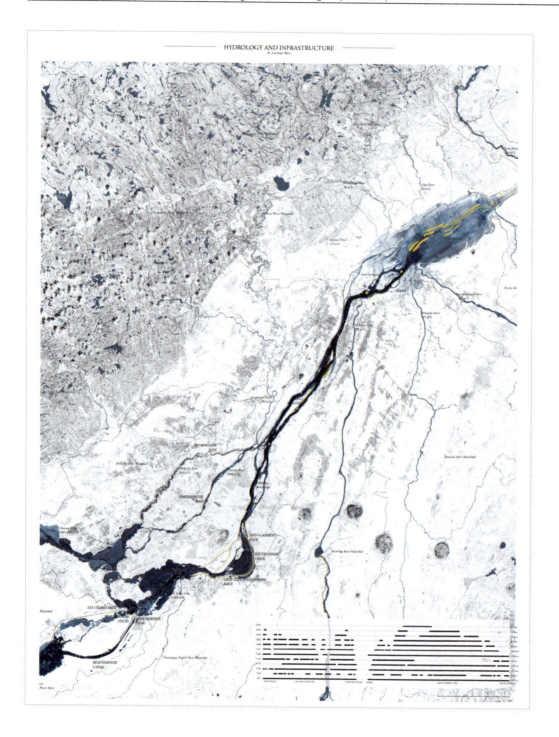

Drawing for Impact—**Case Study Examples**

above and left: Drawing selections from Terre d'eau—Land of Water by Marianne Lafontaine-Chicha.

Visual Communication for Architects and Designers: constructing the persuasive presentation

Drawing selection from 3rd Lab for Visionary Public Design by Annika Babra.

Drawing for Impact—**Case Study Examples**

Drawing selection from A Digital Museum: An Exploration in the Projection of/through Space by Jaron Popko.

Visual Communication for Architects and Designers: constructing the persuasive presentation

Drawing for Impact—**Case Study Examples**

Drawing selection from Futurism 2.0 by Nicolas Turchi.

Visual Communication for Architects and Designers: constructing the persuasive presentation

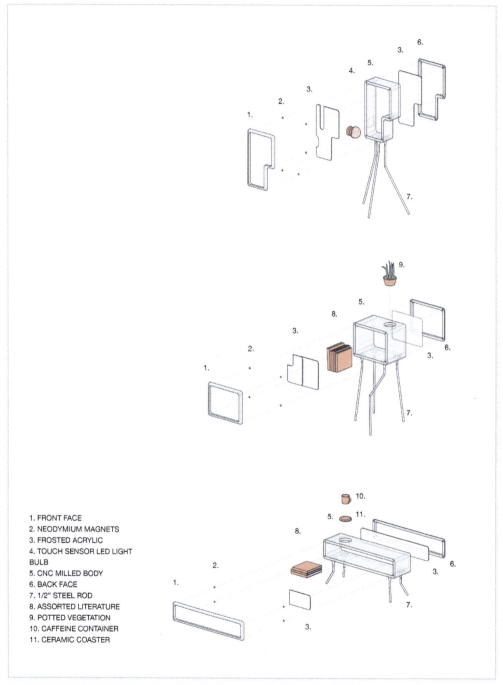

1. FRONT FACE
2. NEODYMIUM MAGNETS
3. FROSTED ACRYLIC
4. TOUCH SENSOR LED LIGHT BULB
5. CNC MILLED BODY
6. BACK FACE
7. 1/2" STEEL ROD
8. ASSORTED LITERATURE
9. POTTED VEGETATION
10. CAFFEINE CONTAINER
11. CERAMIC COASTER

Drawing selection from Furniture: a Lamp, a Bookshelf, a Coffee Table by Natacha Schnider.

Drawing for Impact—**Case Study Examples**

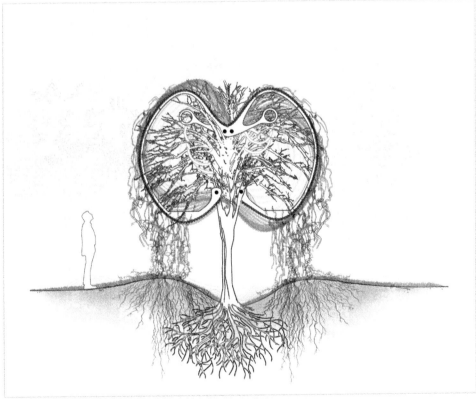

Drawing selections from Carapace by Vruti Desai and Avinash Sharma.

Visual Communication for Architects and Designers: constructing the persuasive presentation

above and right: Drawing selections from American Dreamland by Vardhan Mehta and Braden Young.

Drawing for Impact—**Case Study Examples**

1. Existing Urban Fabric 2. Existing Industries 3. Transit Node - Light Rail, Commerce, Urban parks 4. Apartment Housing 5. Courtyard Housing 6. Urban Farm Housing 7. Industries in Marshland

Notes

Communication, Representation and Presentation

1. Margaret Fletcher, *Constructing the Persuasive Portfolio: The Only Primer You'll Ever Need* (New York and London: Routledge, 2017), 24.

2. Fletcher, *Constructing the Persuasive Portfolio*, 24.

3. Fletcher, 24.

4. Similar principles of design narratives relate to both presentation design and portfolio design. To learn how these principles relate, see Fletcher, *Constructing the Persuasive Portfolio*, 23–5.

Constructing a Visual Argument

1. Discussion of project narrative in presentation design also relates to discussion of project narrative in portfolio design. To understand how this discussion relates to portfolio design, see Fletcher, *Constructing the Persuasive Portfolio*, 120–1.

2. Topics related to finding gaps in the project narrative, the order of the project narrative, the role of primary images and support images relate both to presentations and portfolios. To understand how these topics relate to portfolio design, see Fletcher, *Constructing the Persuasive Portfolio*, 122, 124, 126–7.

3. Fletcher, *Constructing the Persuasive Portfolio*, 74.

4. Fletcher, 75.

5. Fletcher, 79.

6. Image bleeds and the visual relationship between objects on a page have similar properties in both presentation design and portfolio design. To understand how these principles relate to portfolio design, see Fletcher, *Constructing the Persuasive Portfolio*, 80–4.

7. Fletcher, *Constructing the Persuasive Portfolio*, 84.

8. Fletcher, 126.

9. Adjacency relationships, content pairs, content series, chronology content, timeline content, video and film content, four square grids, white space on a page and overlapping content follow similar rules for both presentation design as well as portfolio design. To see how these topics are discussed in relation to portfolios, see Fletcher, *Constructing the Persuasive Portfolio*, 84–9.

10. Fletcher, *Constructing the Persuasive Portfolio*, 95.

11. Location of primary images, the relationship between images and text, visual weight, visual gravity, use of color and balance and symmetry are all concepts that can also relate to portfolio design. For more information on how these concepts relate to portfolio design, see Fletcher, *Constructing the Persuasive Portfolio*, 96–107.

12. Issues of typography apply to both portfolios and presentations. To understand how they relate to portfolios, see Fletcher, *Constructing the Persuasive Portfolio*, 108.

13. Fletcher, *Constructing the Persuasive Portfolio*, 108.

14. Fletcher, 108.

15. Visual issues related to typeface range, typeface legibility, use of upper and lower case, understanding of x-height, kerning, tracking, leading, measure, text alignment, orphans, widows, runts and graphic punctuation are universally the same across presentation design and portfolio design. To better understand how these principles apply to portfolios, see Fletcher, *Constructing the Persuasive Portfolio*, 109–16.

16. Architectural symbols and conventions relate to all graphic representations. To understand how they relate to portfolio design, see Fletcher, *Constructing the Persuasive Portfolio*, 128–30.

17. Principles of labeling systems apply to both presentations and portfolios. To understand how these principles relate to portfolios, see Fletcher, *Constructing the Persuasive Portfolio*, 131–3.

18. Fletcher, *Constructing the Persuasive Portfolio*, 139.

19. Guidelines about contour lines, poché, hatch and compound line edits are similar for both presentations and portfolios. To learn how they relate to portfolios, see Fletcher, *Constructing the Persuasive Portfolio*, 139–40.

20. Fletcher, *Constructing the Persuasive Portfolio*, 140.

21. Fletcher, 142.

22. Floor plate clarity, image quality issues and rich black formula are treated similarly in presentations as in portfolios. To learn how these principles apply to portfolios, see Fletcher, *Constructing the Persuasive Portfolio*, 142–3.

Presentation Design

1. Fletcher, *Constructing the Persuasive Portfolio*, 145.

2. The principle of three levels of reading of a presentation is similar in nature to the three levels of reading of a portfolio. To understand how this principle applies to portfolios, see Fletcher, *Constructing the Persuasive Portfolio*, 121, 123.

3. Principles of writing strategies, graphic presence of text, typeface hierarchy systems, flexibility within a typeface hierarchy system, the balance of graphic hierarchy between image and text and the content and visual goals of text are similarly applied to both presentation design and portfolio design. To understand these similarities, see Fletcher, *Constructing the Persuasive Portfolio*, 146–50.

Presenting Yourself Professionally

1. For additional information on portfolio design and to see other portfolios analyzed in the manner found in this chapter, see Fletcher, *Constructing the Persuasive Portfolio*, 182–239.

2. Fletcher, *Constructing the Persuasive Portfolio*, x–xi.

Acknowledgments

This publication would not have been possible without the enthusiasm of the team at Routledge / Taylor & Francis. In particular, I would like to thank Christine Bondira, Fran Ford, Krystal LaDuc, Julia Pollacco and Alanna Donaldson.

The College of Architecture, Design and Construction at Auburn University has provided immeasurable support for this work. My sincere thanks go to Vini Nathan, Dean and McWhorter Endowed Chair; Christian Dagg, Head of the School of Architecture, Planning and Landscape Architecture at Auburn University; and colleagues Steven K. Wall, Rusty Smith, Justin Miller and Carla Keyvanian.

I'd also like to sincerely thank my family and friends for putting up with another few years of this kind of preoccupation. And to my dear husband, Russ, for his cheerful willingness to constantly rearrange our lives so I had time to work on this project.

I would like to thank all of the designers who responded to my International Presentation Call and submitted work for inclusion in this book. Without their enthusiasm for this project, I wouldn't have had over 50,000 wonderful design examples to make selections from. In particular, I would like to thank the following designers who submitted work to be included in this volume:

Mai Abusalih—University of Khartoum, Columbia University
Kyle Anderson—Auburn University
Jaysen Ariola—University of Manitoba, University of Toronto
Annika Babra—University of Waterloo
Michelle Badr—University of California, Berkeley; Yale University
Paul Bamson—The University of Tennessee, Knoxville; The University of Tennessee, Knoxville
William Baumgardner—Louisiana State University, Harvard Graduate School of Design
Joana Benin—Ryerson University
Hallie Black—Cornell University
Katharine Blackman—University of California, Berkeley; Yale University
Camille Bongard—Architectural Association
Abena Bonna—Wellesley College, Yale University
Anna Budnikova—Kazan State University of Architecture and Engineering, Higher School of Economics
Andrea Bulloni—Politecnico di Milano, Politecnico di Milano
Paul-Andrei Burghelea—University of Greenwich
Alexandra Cabana—University of California, Berkeley
Hawraa Charara—Texas A&M University, Clemson University
Nathan Chen—The University of Texas at Austin
Chang Cheng—Pratt Institute, Columbia University
Guan Yi Chuah—New Jersey Institute of Technology
Gary Chung—University at Buffalo, SUNY; University of Michigan
Liz Clark—Auburn University
Emily Clowes—University of the West of England, University of the West of England
Andrei-Ciprian Cojocaru—University of Greenwich, The Bartlett School of Architecture, UCL
Ece Comert—Istanbul Technical University, Harvard Graduate School of Design
Sam Coulton—The Bartlett School of Architecture, UCL; The Bartlett School of Architecture, UCL
Gaia Crocella—Umeå School of Architecture, Umeå School of Architecture
Chaoyi Cui—Central Academy of Fine Arts, University of Toronto
Adriana F. Davis—New Jersey Institute of Technology, University of Pennsylvania
Lin Derong—National University of Singapore, National University of Singapore
Vruti Desai—Rizvi College of Architecture, Pratt Institute
K. Michelle Doll—The University of Texas at San Antonio, University of Houston
Caroline Dunn—California Polytechnic State University, San Luis Obispo
Catherine Earley—Virginia Polytechnic Institute and State University, University of Oregon
Daniel Elkington—University of Lincoln, University of Lincoln
Stephanie Elward—University of Portsmouth, University of Kent
Wei Fan—Qingdao University of Technology, The University of Melbourne
Eilis Finnegan—Auburn University
Annalaura Fornasier—Arts University Bournemouth
Cameron Foster—Portland State University, Clemson University
Andie Gamble—Auburn University
Eric Giragosian—Woodbury University, Columbia University
Charlie Glenton—University of Plymouth, University of Plymouth
Fernanda García Gregori—Universidad Anáhuac México
Danny Griffin—Georgia Institute of Technology
Chenyuan Gu—Ball State University, Harvard Graduate School of Design
Julia Hager—Virginia Polytechnic Institute and State University
William Hall—Auburn University
Alexander Michael Hamady—Auburn University
Samantha Hamilton—Birmingham City University, University of Plymouth
Ayah Hatahet—Leeds Beckett University, Leeds Beckett University
Benjamin Hayes—University of Bath, Harvard Graduate School of Design
Min He—Rensselaer Polytechnic Institute, Columbia University
Andrew Hong—The University of Texas at Austin
Kuan Chieh Huang—Tamkang University, Manchester School of Architecture
Catalina Elena Ionita—University of Huddersfield, Sheffield Hallam University
Mariam Jacob—American University of Sharjah
Anna Jankowska—Białystok University of Technology, Białystok University of Technology
Joel Jassu—The University of Memphis, Georgia Institute of Technology
Mariama M.M. Kah—American University of Sharjah
Berke Kalemoglu—Auburn University, Columbia University
Jaclyn Kaloczi—Ontario College of Art and Design University, The University of British Columbia
Rasem Kamal—The University of Jordan, Rice University
Jianan Kang—Tianjin Chengjian University, Georgia Institute of Technology
Yifu Kang—University of Oregon, Cornell University

Visual Communication for Architects and Designers: constructing the persuasive presentation

Mert Kansu—Bahçeşehir University, The University of Virginia
Carson Keeney—Auburn University
Gretchen Kelly—University of Kansas, University of Kansas
Nada Khalaf—American University of Sharjah
Kurt Kimsey—Marywood University
Clay Kiningham—Georgia Institute of Technology, Georgia Institute of Technology
Elena Koepp—Arizona State University, University of Oregon
Katie Koskey—Georgia Institute of Technology, Massachusetts Institute of Technology
Riley Lacalli—University of Washington, Tulane University
Alexandra Lacatusu—University of Kent, Oxford Brookes University
Marianne Lafontaine-Chicha—University of Toronto
Alitsia Lambrianidou—University of Plymouth, University of Plymouth
Zoe Latham—University of Plymouth, University of Plymouth
Tate Lauderdale—Auburn University
Donguk Lee—Louisiana State University
Je Sung Lee—Kookmin University, Harvard Graduate School of Design
Samuel Letchford—Nottingham Trent University, University of Sheffield
Stanley Ka Chun Leung—Central Saint Martins, Savannah College of Art and Design
Meikang Li—Shandong University of Architecture and Engineering, University of Toronto
Jing Liao—University of Waterloo
Kaiying Lin—Southern California Institute of Architecture
Wei Lin—Southern Illinois University Carbondale, University of Illinois Urbana-Champaign
Shi Yin Ling—The Bartlett School of Architecture, UCL
Fergus Littlejohn—Northumbria University, University of Kent
Chang Liu—The Ohio State University
Alexis Luna—New Jersey Institute of Technology, New Jersey Institute of Technology
Natalia Sabrina Ortiz Luna—University of Nebraska–Lincoln, University of Oregon
Xiaodan Ma—Syracuse University, Columbia University
Prakash Maharjan—Tribhuvan University
Roberto Diaz Manzanares—Texas A&M University, Clemson University
James Mason—London South Bank University
Chris McAvoy—Ulster University, Ulster University
Trey McMillon—Georgia Institute of Technology, Virginia Polytechnic Institute and State University
Ruth McNickle—The University of Edinburgh, The University of Edinburgh
Vardhan Mehta—Pratt Institute, Harvard Graduate School of Design
Jennifer Minor—Texas A&M University, University of Houston
Victor Moldoveanu—Aarhus School of Architecture
Andrea del Pilar Monroig-Torres—Pontifical Catholic University of Puerto Rico, Pratt Institute
Abraham Murrell—The University of Maryland, Columbia University
Margaret Ndungu—London Metropolitan University, De Montfort University

Aaron Neal—Auburn University
Gaurav Neupane—Tribhuvan University, Kansas State University
George Newton—University of Nottingham
Chit Yee Ng—New Jersey Institute of Technology, New Jersey Institute of Technology
Caroline Niederpruem—University at Buffalo, SUNY; Cornell University
Francisco Ramos Ordóñez—University of Seville, Harvard Graduate School of Design
Marwah Osama—American University of Sharjah
Caitlin Owens—University College Cork, University College Cork
Edward Palka—University of Minnesota, Columbia University
Marco Papagni—Politecnico di Milano
Paresh Parmar—University for the Creative Arts, University of Westminster
Maria Pastorelli—Georgia Institute of Technology, Georgia Institute of Technology
Julie Pierides—Georgia Institute of Technology
Derek Pirozzi—University of South Florida School of Architecture and Community Design
Eva Pontika—University of Plymouth, University of Plymouth
Jaron Popko—University of Cincinnati, University of Cincinnati
Meghan Quigley—University of Illinois at Chicago, University of Illinois at Chicago
Sahr Qureishi—University of Nebraska–Lincoln
Phil Riazzi—University of Cincinnati, Clemson University
Helena Rong—Cornell University, Massachusetts Institute of Technology
Daniel Rose—The University of Tennessee, Knoxville; The University of Tennessee, Knoxville
Meghan Royster—University of Michigan, Yale University
Barbara Ruech—University of Liechtenstein, University of Liechtenstein
Petra Salameh—University of Houston
Alberto de Salvatierra—Cornell University, Harvard Graduate School of Design
Henry Savoie—Auburn University
Hannah Schafers—University of Nebraska–Lincoln, University of Nebraska–Lincoln
Natacha Schnider—California Polytechnic State University, San Luis Obispo
Will Shadwick—University of Kansas, University of Kansas
Li Shan—Shandong Jianzhu University
Avinash Sharma—Rizvi College of Architecture, Pratt Institute
Xiwei Shen—Louisiana State University, Harvard Graduate School of Design
Sanjeev Shrestha—Tribhuvan University
Dovydas Simkus—Northumbria University, The University of Sheffield
Prakhar Singh—Auburn University
Ty Skeiky—Maryland Institute College of Art
Qiwei Song—Zhejiang A&F University, University of Toronto
Chella Strong—Pitzer College, Harvard Graduate School of Design
Neely Sutter—University of Nebraska–Lincoln, University of Nebraska–Lincoln
Ward Taliaferro—Auburn University
Sajan Tamrakar—Tribhuvan University

Notes / Acknowledgments

Stephanie Tang—University of California, Berkeley
Kyle Taveira—Temple University, Temple University
Billy Taylor—London South Bank University, Oxford Brookes University
Dustin Toothman—Fairmont State University; The University of Tennessee, Knoxville
Chau Tran—New Jersey Institute of Technology, New Jersey Institute of Technology
Sarah Treherne—University of the Witwatersrand, University of Johannesburg
Nicolas Turchi—University of Bologna, Harvard Graduate School of Design
Gege Wang—Peking University, Harvard Graduate School of Design
Lauren Wertz—Auburn University
Matthew Wieber—Marywood University
Matthew Williams—Kennesaw State University
Shuailin Wu—Beijing Forestry University, Washington University in St. Louis
Kelsey Wynne—Auburn University
Boyu Xiao—Auburn University
Zhicheng Xu—Purdue University, Massachusetts Institute of Technology
Cherry Yang—Rhode Island School of Design
Sun Yen Yee—Newcastle University, University of Westminster
Kayli Yentzen—Texas A&M University, University of Houston
Dongkyu Yoon—Auburn University
Braden Young—Pratt Institute
Katarina Zatkova—University of Liverpool, University of Cambridge
Dandi Zhang—Iowa State University, Harvard Graduate School of Design
Jiaoyue Zhao—The University of Liverpool, Southern California Institute of Architecture
Jingxiao Zhou—The Ohio State University

Work in this volume includes examples by over 180 designers from 130 different schools representing 24 countries from North America, South America, Europe, the Middle East, Asia, Oceania and Africa.

The visual content for this publication was selected from over 50,000 images submitted for possible inclusion. The final 750 examples offer a detailed view of the work happening around the world at the time of publishing. Students studying in the following countries are represented in the work found in this publication: Australia, Canada, China, Denmark, India, Ireland, Italy, Jordan, Liechtenstein, Mexico, Nepal, Poland, Russia, Singapore, South Africa, South Korea, Spain, Sweden, Sudan, Taiwan, Turkey, the United Arab Emirates, the United Kingdom and the United States of America.

Visual Communication for Architects and Designers: constructing the persuasive presentation

Illustration Credits

Mai Abusalih 82
Kyle Anderson 245
Jaysen Ariola 176–7
Annika Babra 24–5, 268
Michelle Badr 248–9
Paul Bamson 124
William Baumgardner 244
Joana Benin 140–5
Hallie Black 261
Katharine Blackman 248–9
Camille Bongard 211
Abena Bonna 83
Anna Budnikova 26
Andrea Bulloni 58
Paul-Andrei Burghelea 73
Alexandra Cabana 226–7
Hawraa Charara 63
Nathan Chen 03
Chang Cheng 184–5
Guan Yi Chuah 55
Gary Chung 260
Liz Clark 53
Emily Clowes 199
Andrei-Ciprian Cojocaru 106–7
Ece Comert 96
Sam Coulton 182–3
Gaia Crocella 64–5
Chaoyi Cui 94–5
Adriana F. Davis 220–1
Lin Derong 238–9
Vruti Desai 273
K. Michelle Doll 104
Caroline Dunn 198
Catherine Earley 32
Daniel Elkington 250
Stephanie Elward 262–3
Wei Fan 94
Maria Faraone 222–3
Eilis Finnegan 241
Annalaura Fornasier 244
Cameron Foster 31
Andie Gamble 60
Eric Giragosian 82
Charlie Glenton 234–7
Fernanda García Gregori 187
Danny Griffin 232
Chenyuan Gu 244
Julia Hager 07
William Hall 160–5
Alexander Michael Hamady 67
Samantha Hamilton 234–7
Ayah Hatahet 76, 89
Benjamin Hayes 96
Min He 82
Andrew Hong 03, 195
Kuan Chieh Huang 97
Michael Hughes 170–3

Catalina Elena Ionita 92–3
Mariam Jacob 133
Anna Jankowska 228–9
Joel Jassu 23
Mariama M.M. Kah 258–9
Berke Kalemoglu 174–5
Jaclyn Kaloczi 18–19
Rasem Kamal 180–1
Jianan Kang 52, 154–5
Yifu Kang 108–9
Mert Kansu 29
Carson Keeney 60
Gretchen Kelly 112–13
Nada Khalaf 91, 133
Kurt Kimsey 36–7
Clay Kiningham 30, 231
Elena Koepp 32
Katie Koskey 225, 232
Riley Lacalli 214–15
Alexandra Lacatusu 222–3
Marianne Lafontaine-Chicha 266–7
Mani Lall 45
Alitsia Lambrianidou 194
Zoe Latham 194
Tate Lauderdale 60
Donguk Lee 68
Je Sung Lee 40–1
Samuel Letchford 78–9
Stanley Ka Chun Leung 216–17
Meikang Li 94–5
Jing Liao 233
Kaiying Lin 125
Wei Lin 46
Shi Yin Ling 202–3
Fergus Littlejohn 188–9
Chang Liu 230
Alexis Luna 55
Natalia Sabrina Ortiz Luna 32
Xiaodan Ma 184–5
Prakash Maharjan 186
Roberto Diaz Manzanares 63
James Mason 77
Chris McAvoy 192
Trey McMillon 224
Ruth McNickle 56–7
Vardhan Mehta 274–5
Fernando Menis 170–3
Jennifer Minor 104
Victor Moldoveanu 252–5
Andrea del Pilar Monroig-Torres 54
Abraham Murrell 81
Margaret Ndungu 178–9
Aaron Neal 102
Gaurav Neupane 186
George Newton 45
Chit Yee Ng 55
Zui Ng 104

Illustration Credits

Caroline Niederpruem 84
Francisco Ramos Ordóñez 208–9
Marwah Osama 170–3
Caitlin Owens 212–13
Edward Palka 81
Marco Papagni 58
Paresh Parmar 205
Maria Pastorelli 30
Owen Hughes Pearce 222–3
Julie Pierides 30
Derek Pirozzi 120–1
Eva Pontika 234–7
Jaron Popko 269
Meghan Quigley 13, 210
Sahr Qureishi 50
Phil Riazzi 31
Helena Rong 05, 257
Daniel Rose 206–7
Meghan Royster 242–3, 264–5
Barbara Ruech 200
Petra Salameh 256
Alberto de Salvatierra 48–9
Henry Savoie 39, 146–53
Hannah Schafers 168–9
Natacha Schnider 272
Will Shadwick 112–13
Li Shan 201
Avinash Sharma 273
Xiwei Shen 68
Toby Shew 222–3
Sanjeev Shrestha 186
Dovydas Simkus 90
Prakhar Singh 67
Ty Skeiky 193
Qiwei Song 94–5
Chella Strong 48–9
Neely Sutter 17
Ward Taliaferro 51
Sajan Tamrakar 186
Stephanie Tang 190–1
Kyle Taveira 101
Billy Taylor 218–19
Dustin Toothman 206–7
Chau Tran 251
Sarah Treherne 204
Nicolas Turchi 270–1
Gege Wang 48–9
Lauren Wertz 103
Matthew Wieber 36–7, 105
Matthew Williams 27
Shuailin Wu 123
Kelsey Wynne 60
Boyu Xiao 67
Zhicheng Xu 246–7
Cherry Yang 240
Sun Yen Yee 196–7
Kayli Yentzen 104

Dongkyu Yoon 67
Braden Young 274–5
Katarina Zatkova 75
Dandi Zhang 244
Jiaoyue Zhao 125
Jingxiao Zhou 230

Cover Art: *line field 1:3* by Margaret Fletcher, archival ink on Arches 140 hotpress paper. Courtesy of the author.

Visual Communication for Architects and Designers: constructing the persuasive presentation

Index

A Abusalih, Mai 82
active area 21, 28–9, 100, 131
adjacency 12, 21, 33–5, 47
  caption 35, 121
  chronology 35
  pairs 34
  series 34
  sets 34
  text 121
  timeline 35
  title 35
alignment
  image 33–4
  system(s) 13, 21–5, 100
  text 62, 65–6
  vertical 62, 66
Anderson, Kyle 245
argument
  building an 131–2
  complex 88–92, 131
  verbal 03, 117–19
  visual ix, 15–19, 44–7, 100, 128, 130
  written 117–19
Ariola, Jaysen 176–7
arrow(s) 82–3
  north 72
audience 02, 06–7, 138

B Babra, Annika 24–5, 268
background 38, 100–3, 109
Badr, Michelle 248–9
balance 57–9, 121
  visual 50
Bamson, Paul 124
baseline(s) 21–4, 28
Baumgardner, William 244
Benin, Joana 140–5
Black, Hallie 261
Blackman, Katharine 248–9
bleed(s) 29–30
blind review 06, 92–3, 116–17, 130–1
board(s)
  challenges 106–8
  designing 08–9, 99–113
  layout 22–5, 28
  multiple 38–9
  organization 100–105
  printed 93–4
  proportions 106–8
  setup 110
  submission 110–11
body text 61, 116, 119–22
bold 61–2, 119–20
Bongard, Camille 211
Bonna, Abena 83
Budnikova, Anna 26
bullets 69
Bulloni, Andrea 58
Burghelea, Paul-Andrei 73

C Cabana, Alexandra 226–7
call-outs 73–9, 119–25
captions 35, 116–22
case study 167–275
Charara, Hawraa 63
Chen, Nathan 03
Cheng, Chang 184–5
Chuah, Guan Yi 55
Chung, Gary 260
Clark, Liz 53
Clowes, Emily 199
Cojocaru, Andrei-Ciprian 106–7
color
  cohesion 51
  highlight 54–5
  in presentation 50–7
  matching 52–4
  systems 51–2
  vibration 132
column width 25
Comert, Ece 96
communication design 01–3, 07
competitions 92, 106, 130–1
Constructing the Persuasive Portfolio ix, 135
contour lines 80
conventions, drawing 71–85
correspondence 135–7
Coulton, Sam 182–3
cover letters 136
Crocella, Gaia 64–5
Cui, Chaoyi 94–5

D dashes 69
Davis, Adriana F. 220–1
Derong, Lin 238–9
Desai, Vruti 273
design
  communication 01–3, 07
  directional 100
  narrative 08, 11–13
  presentation 01, 06–7
  representation 01, 04–5, 07
  zone 100
designer, hand of 04
diagram
  labels 61, 74–5, 117, 119–25
  shaped 109
digital
  presentation(s) 44, 72, 87–8, 131–3
  slide deck(s) 09, 88, 93–4, 131–3
  wayfinding 132
Doll, K. Michelle 104
door swings 83–4
drawing
  conventions 71–85
  for impact 167–275
  labels 61, 74–5, 117, 119–25
Dunn, Caroline 198

282

Index

E Earley, Catherine 32
Elkington, Daniel 250
ellipsis 69
Elward, Stephanie 262–3
em dash 69
en dash 69
eye level 103–5

F Fan, Wei 94
Faraone, Maria 222–3
feedback 02–3
film 35, 40–1
Finnegan, Eilis 241
foreground 38–9, 100–3, 109
Fornasier, Annalaura 244
Foster, Cameron 31

G Gamble, Andie 60
Giragosian, Eric 82
Glenton, Charlie 234–7
graphic
  design 43
  punctuation 69
  scale 72
Gregori, Fernanda García 187
grid
  compound 22–4
  modular 22
  system 22–5
Griffin, Danny 232
Gu, Chenyuan 244

H Hager, Julia 07
Hall, William 160–5
Hamady, Alexander Michael 67
Hamilton, Samantha 234–7
hands 129
hanglines 22–4
Hatahet, Ayah 76, 89
hatch 81
Hayes, Benjamin 96
He, Min 82
hierarchy
  typeface 59–64, 74, 119–21
  visual 18–19, 33–4, 39, 44–7
Hong, Andrew 03, 195
Huang, Kuan Chieh 97
Hughes, Michael 170–3
hyphen 66, 69

I ideas, organizing 118–19
image(s)
  focus 85
  primary 18–19, 33–4, 44–7
  size of 33–4
  support 18–19
  quality 85
ink 110

in-person review 11–12, 92–3, 103–5, 128–30
Ionita, Catalina Elena 92–3
italics 62

J Jacob, Mariam 133
Jankowska, Anna 228–9
Jassu, Joel 23
justification 65–6, 119

K Kah, Mariama M.M. 258–9
Kalemoglu, Berke 174–5
Kaloczi, Jaclyn 18–19
Kamal, Rasem 180–1
Kang, Jianan 52, 154–9
Kang, Yifu 108–9
Kansu, Mert 29
Keeney, Carson 60
Kelly, Gretchen 112–13
kerning 62–4
Khalaf, Nada 91, 133
Kimsey, Kurt 36–7
Kiningham, Clay 30, 231
Koepp, Elena 32
Koskey, Katie 225, 232

L label(s)
  diagram 61, 74–5, 117, 119–25
  drawing 61, 74–5, 117, 119–25
  plan 74–5
  secondary 75
  systems 74–5
Lacalli, Riley 214–15
Lacatusu, Alexandra 222–3
Lafontaine-Chicha, Marianne 266–7
Lall, Mani 45
Lambrianidou, Alitsia 194
Latham, Zoe 194
Lauderdale, Tate 60
leader lines 73–9, 125
leading 62–4, 69
Lee, Donguk 68
Lee, Je Sung 40–1
Letchford, Samuel 78–9
Leung, Stanley Ka Chun 216–17
Li, Meikang 94–5
Liao, Jing 233
Lin, Kaiying 125
Lin, Wei 46
line
  compound 81–2
  contour 80
  weight 80
  work 85
Ling, Shi Yin 202–3
Littlejohn, Fergus 188–9
Liu, Chang 230
lowercase 62
Luna, Alexis 55
Luna, Natalia Sabrina Ortiz 32

Visual Communication for Architects and Designers: constructing the persuasive presentation

M
Ma, Xiaodan 184–5
Maharjan, Prakash 186
Manzanares, Roberto Diaz 63
margins 22–4, 28–35
Mason, James 77
McAvoy, Chris 192
McMillon, Trey 224
McNickle, Ruth 56–7
measure 64–5
Mehta, Vardhan 274–5
Menis, Fernando 170–3
message 02–7, 33, 117, 128
middle ground 38–9, 100–3, 109
Minor, Jennifer 104
Moldoveanu, Victor 252–5
Monroig-Torres, Andrea del Pilar 54
Murrell, Abraham 81

N
narrative
 design 11–13
 presentation 12, 87–97
 project 12–13, 15–19
 visual 12–13, 21–41
Ndungu, Margaret 178–9
Neal, Aaron 102
Neupane, Gaurav 186
Newton, George 45
Ng, Chit Yee 55
Ng, Zui 104
Niederpruem, Caroline 84

O
Ordóñez, Francisco Ramos 208–9
organization
 board 100–5
 logical 06
 portfolio 138
 visual 21–41
orphan 66
Osama, Marwah 170–3
overlapping content 38, 47, 103
Owens, Caitlin 212–13

P
Palka, Edward 81
Papagni, Marco 58
paper 110
Parmar, Paresh 205
Pastorelli, Maria 30
pdf
 exporting 111
 optimizing 111
 resolution 111
Pearce, Owen Hughes 222–3
Pierides, Julie 30
Pirozzi, Derek 120–1
plan
 labels 74–5
poché 80–3

Pontika, Eva 234–7
Popko, Jaron 269
portfolios 135
 design actions 138–9
 examples of 140–65
presentation
 boards 99–113
 constructing a 19, 24–5
 design 01, 06–9
 digital 44, 72, 85, 87–8, 131–3
 drawings 80–4
 in-person 11–12, 92–3, 103–5, 128–30
 narrative 12, 87–97
 notes 128–9
 practice 07, 128–9
 start designing 08–9, 24–5
 strategies 100–5, 127–33
 testing 07, 130–3
project narrative 12–13, 15–19
 gaps 16–17
 order 17–18

Q
Quigley, Meghan 13, 210
Qureishi, Sahr 50

R
representation design 01, 04–5, 07
resume(s) 135–7
review(s)
 blind 06, 92–3, 116–17, 130–1
 in-person 11–12, 92–3, 103–5, 128–30
Riazzi, Phil 31
rich black 85
Rong, Helena 05, 257
Rose, Daniel 206–7
Royster, Meghan 242–3, 264–5
Ruech, Barbara 200
runt 66

S
Salameh, Petra 256
Salvatierra, Alberto de 48–9
sans serif typeface 61–2, 119
Savoie, Henry 39, 146–53
Schafers, Hannah 168–9
Schnider, Natacha 272
section cut lines 72–3
serif typeface 61–2, 119
Shadwick, Will 112–13
Shan, Li 201
Sharma, Avinash 273
Shen, Xiwei 68
Shew, Toby 222–3
Shrestha, Sanjeev 186
signs 04
Simkus, Dovydas 90
Singh, Prakhar 67
Skeiky, Ty 193
slide deck 09, 88, 93–4, 131–3

284

Index

software 09, 80, 85, 110–11
Song, Qiwei 94–5
strategies
   board organization 100–5
   portfolios 138
   presentation 100–5, 127–33
   verbal 117–19
   written 117–19
Strong, Chella 48–9
subtitle 61, 116–22
Sutter, Neely 17
symbols 02, 04, 71–4
symmetry 57–9

T Taliaferro, Ward 51
Tamrakar, Sajan 186
Tang, Stephanie 190–1
Taveira, Kyle 101
Taylor, Billy 218–19
tee-up set 09
text 115–25
   alignment 65–6
   width 64–5
title 61, 116–22
Toothman, Dustin 206–7
tracking 62–6
Tran, Chau 251
Treherne, Sarah 204
Turchi, Nicolas 270–1
typeface
   hierarchy 59–64, 74, 119–21
   range 61, 119
   sans serif 61–2, 119
   selection 61–2, 119, 131
   serif 61–2, 119
typography, graphic rules of 59–66

U underline 62, 120
uppercase 62

V verbal strategies 117–19
video 35, 88, 132
visual
   argument ix, 15–19, 44–7, 100, 128, 130
   gravity 28, 49–50
   hierarchy 18–19, 33–4, 39, 44–7
   legibility 33–4, 61–2, 80
   narrative 12–13, 21–41
   order 21, 39, 44–50
   organization 21–41
   reading 116–17
   relationship 33–9, 100, 120
   stickiness 33
   structure 21–41
   weight 47–50

W Wang, Gege 48–9
wayfinding, digital 132
Wertz, Lauren 103

white space 28, 35–8
widow 66
Wieber, Matthew 36–7, 105
Williams, Matthew 27
words, value of 117–19
written strategies 117–19
Wu, Shuailin 123
Wynne, Kelsey 60

X x-height 62
Xiao, Boyu 67
Xu, Zhicheng 246–7

Y Yang, Cherry 240
Yee, Sun Yen 196–7
Yentzen, Kayli 104
Yoon, Dongkyu 67
Young, Braden 274–5

Z Zatkova, Katarina 75
Zhang, Dandi 244
Zhao, Jiaoyue 125
Zhou, Jingxiao 230

Colophon

Futura designed by Paul Renner, 1927.
Helvetica Neue originally designed by Max Miedinger, 1957; redesigned by D. Stempel AG, 1983.
Gill Sans designed by Eric Gill, 1928.